ASIAN BABIES' NAMES
FROM THE HINDU, MUSLIM AND SIKH TRADITIONS

ASIAN BABIES' NAMES

From the Hindu, Muslim and Sikh Traditions

Sachin and Sonal Parekh

RIGHT WAY

Copyright notice

Typeset in 10pt Times by Letterpart Ltd., Reigate, Surrey.
Printed and bound in Great Britain by Cox & Wyman Ltd., Reading, Berkshire.

The *Right Way* series is published by Elliot Right Way Books, Brighton Road, Lower Kingswood, Tadworth, Surrey, KT20 6TD, U.K. For information about our company and the other books we publish, visit our website at www.right-way.co.uk

CONTENTS

DEDICATION

This book is dedicated to our parents who gave us our wonderful names and meaning to our lives.

Introduction

A name represents a person's identity, and is the individualism by which he/she is known and singled out. As such, one of the most important pleasures parents have is to choose a name for their child. Often, a name which has a cultural or ethnic significance is important, although the most popular names may also have a modern touch, or a relevant meaning.

The Indian sub-continent is a land of great diversity. It is the birthplace of many religions. The people inherited a civilization that began more than 4,500 years ago, one that has proven capable of absorbing and transforming the people and cultures that over the centuries have come to the sub-continent. There are 17 major languages and 844 dialects. Parents from different ethnic origins have different tastes for the names of their children, as well as varying methods of choosing these names. This book is an attempt to assist parents of various religions, languages and regions in selecting the appropriate name, by broadly classifying the names as Hindu, Muslim and Sikh. However, there is no intention to make any racial division.

India's population is rich with diverse ethnic as well as cultural groups. Ethnic groups are those based on a sense of common ancestry, while cultural groups can be made up of people of different ethnic origins who share a common language or beliefs. There is an excessive overlap of names within these ethnic and cultural groups, hence these names are included as Hindu. Hindu (Hindustan) was primarily a geographical term that referred to India as long ago as the sixth century BC. Thus the Hindu names include the following:

- **Hindus:** It is generally believed that the basic tenet of Hinduism was brought to India by the Aryans who settled along the banks of the Indus river. The Hindu tradition encourages Hindus to seek spiritual and moral truth.

- **Jains:** Jain is one of the oldest religions, and upholds non-violence as its supreme principle (Ahimsa Paramo Dharma) and insists upon its observance in thought, word and deed at the individual as well as social levels.

- **Buddhists:** Buddhism is a major world religion. Founded in north-eastern India, it is based on the teachings of Siddhartha Gautama who is known as the Buddha or Enlightened One. Buddhists control their minds and follow the spiritual path to liberation and enlightenment.

- **Bangla/Bengali:** Bangla is the state language of Bangladesh and one of the languages listed in the Indian Constitution. Bangla speakers number about 230 million today.

How To Select A Baby's Name

Many factors influence parents' decisions about what name to give to their child. Prioritisation of these factors, and the weight of consideration given to each of them, is an individual decision. The factors to look at are:

- *Meaning of the name*

  All parents wish their child to have the best qualities. The meaning of the child's name therefore acquires great significance as it reflects the character and qualities of the individual.

- *Pronunciation*

  As well as being easy to pronounce, the name should be one that is pleasant to hear.

- *Ethnic origin/significance of the name*

- *Religious value*

  Many names have religious significance – they may be mentioned in religious books, or be part of religious messages.

- *Historical significance*

- *Fame*

  The fame and success associated with the names of famous personalities (or their children) makes them particularly popular, as parents hope their children will reach similar heights of success.

- *Family traditions*

  Names can often be passed down through generations i.e. from grandfather, to father, to son.

- *Numerology*

    Parents consider various combinations of name (with or without last name, middle name or middle initial) and see which is luckiest. The numbers indicate whether a name is lucky, average, or not so lucky. This method is also used for company names, brand names, etc.

Notes

1. Names marked with '*' (star) are among the top 2,000 baby names in a recent year in the United Kingdom.

2. Names marked with '#' (hash) are also in lists of twin names.

Hindu Names

Astrology is one of the most significant factors in naming a Hindu baby. It is based on Zodiac signs, or Hindu 'Rashi'. There are 12 Hindu Rashis and each Rashi has a letter (or letters) associated with it. According to Hindu tradition, a baby belonging to a particular Rashi should have a name commencing with one of the letters of that Rashi. Please find below a table containing the name of each Rashi, and the letters associated with it.

Rashi	Associated letter/s
Mesh	A, L, E, I
Vrushabh	B, V, U
Mithun	K, CH, GH
Kark	DD, H
Sinh	M, TT
Kanya	P, TTH, N
Tula	R, T
Vrushik	N, Y
Dhan	BH, DH, PH, DDH
Makar	KH, J
Kumbh	G, SH, S
Meen	D, CH, Z, TH

Hindu Boys' Names

A

*#Abhay: Fearless; 'bhay' means 'fear', and adding an 'a' negates the meaning, thus meaning no fear, or fearless

Abhijeet/Abhijit: One who is victorious; has conquered; another name for Lord Vishnu

Abhinav: New; modern; young; fresh

*Abhishek: Shower of milk/water over an idol (a Hindu way of worshipping)

Adarsh: Principles; ideals

Adesh/Aadesh: Voice; impulsion; command

*Aditya/Aaditya: Sun; 'Veda Adityas' are solar Gods, children of infinity i.e. *Aditi;* Aditya is the chairman of the Birla group, one of India's largest business houses

Advait: Exceptional; unique; individual; from the Sanskrit word 'dvai' which means 'two', the addition of the letter 'a' at the beginning of the word negates the meaning, thus meaning non-duality

*#Ajay: Unconquerable; 'jay' means 'victorious' or 'conqueror' – adding an 'a' gives its antonym, thus meaning one who cannot be conquered

*#Akash/Aakash: Sky; ether; space; one of the five *bhuta*s (the fundamental principle of life and the formation of the world); the five elemental states of a substance are aakash (sky), vayu (air), agni/tejas (fire), apas/jala (water) and prithvi (earth)

*#Akhil: Complete; whole

Akhilesh: Lord of the universe; immortal; indestructible

*#Akshay: Immortal; longlived

*Amar: Forever; immortal

Ameya: Boundless; incomprehensible; immeasurable

Amish: Honest; truthful; sincere

***#Amit**: Endless; boundless; unlimited; infinite; another name for Lord Ganesh

Amitabh: One with boundless splendour; Amitabh Bachchan is one of the greatest actors of Bollywood and has lived up to his name! In a recent poll by Channel 4 (UK) to find the 100 greatest stars of all time, Amitabh Bachchan stood alongside actors such as Tom Hanks, Sean Connery, Al Pacino and Robert DeNiro

Amol: Priceless; valuable

***Anand**: Bliss; happiness; pleasure; joy

Anay: Answer of God; Radha's husband

***#Anil**: God of wind

#Aniruddha: Co-operative; something that cannot be restricted; grandson of God Krishna and son of Pradyumna, the God of love

***Anish**: One who has no superior; supreme; another name for Lord Vishnu

***Anmol**: Precious; valuable; dear; loved

***#Anuj**: One born later; younger brother

***#Anup**: Unequalled; unique; boundless in water

#Anurag: Attachment; devotion; love

***Arjun**: White; made of silver; pure; clear; fair complexioned; the third of the Pandavas; husband of Draupadi; Lord Krishna drove Arjun's chariot during the Mahabharata war

Arnav: Ocean; sea

***#Arun**: Sun; red; one of the 12 Adityas

***Arya**: Honoured; respected; kind; devoted; dear

***Aryan/Aryaan**: Noble; dignified; an ancient race

Ashish/Aashish: Blessing; benediction

#Ashok/Ashoka: Originally from the word 'shok' meaning 'sorrow', the letter 'a' at the beginning gives its antonym, thus meaning without sorrow; the Ashoka chakra, 'the wheel of law'

(Dharma chakra), is part of the Indian national flag and the Indian national emblem; the Mauryan emperor, Ashoka, developed the 14ft high Ashoka Pillar in the third century. It was a gift to Delhi from the third Sultan of the Tughlak dynasty, Firoz Shah Tughlak; Ashoka was one of the greatest emperors known to Indian history. He was the grandson of Chandragupta Maurya and the son of Bindusar. The land he ruled stretched from the Himalayas, Nepal and Kashmir to Mysore in the south, from Afghanistan in the north east to the banks of the River Brahmaputra in the east, and in the west his territory covered Saurashtra and Junagarh; Ashoka is one of the most legendary and sacred trees of India, and one of the most fascinating flowers in the Indian range of flower essences. It is found in the central and eastern Himalayas as well as on the west coast of Mumbai. The Hindus regard it as sacred, being dedicated to Kama Deva, God of love. The tree is a symbol of love. Lord Buddha was born under the Ashoka tree, so it is planted in Buddhist monasteries. Parts of this tree are used as medical remedies against many diseases

*Ashwin/Ashvin: One who mounts a horse; a horse rider; derived from the word 'ashva' which means 'horse'; the Vedic God of agriculture; the picture for the zodiac sign of Gemini

Atul: Matchless; incomparable

Avinash: Indestructible; immortal; unconquerable; from the word 'vinash' meaning 'destruction', an 'a' at the beginning gives the antonym – indestructible

*#Ayush: Longlived; age; duration of life

B

Badal: Cloud

Bakul: Flowering tree

Balaji: Strong; powerful; the sacred shrine of Lord Venkateswara–Balaji is the richest shrine in Asia; another name for Lord Vishnu

Balchandra: Young moon; crescent moon; derived by combining two words 'bala' and 'chandra' meaning 'young' and 'moon' respectively

Balgopal: Young cowherd; infant Lord Krishna; from two words, 'bala' and 'gopal' meaning 'young' and 'cowherd' respectively

Barun: Lord of the sea

Bharadwaj: One with swiftness and vigour; name of a singing bird; a sage

Bharat: One who fulfils all desires; brother of Lord Rama; Sanskrit name for India

Bhaskar: Sun; fire; one that gives light; another name for Lord Shiva

Bhaumik: Lord of the earth; belonging to the earth

*Bhavesh: One who exists everywhere; another name for Lord Shiva

Bhavin: Human; living being

Bhupad: Firm; stable; fixed

Bhupendra: Emperor; King of Kings

Bhushan: Adornment; ornaments

Bhuvan: Home; earth

Bipin: Forest

Biren: Lord of warriors

Brijesh: King of nature, derived from the word 'brij' which means 'nature'; another name for Lord Krishna

Buddha: Enlightened; Prince Gautama was called Lord Buddha for his enlightenment and preachings; Lord Buddha was the founder of the Buddhist religion

Budhil: Learned; intelligent; clever

C

Chahel: Good cheer

Chaitanya: Life; liveliness; knowledge; famous sage

Champak: White flower; the name of a tree

Chanakya: Bright; witty; Chanakya was the minister of Chandragupta Maurya and was famous for his tactical mind

Chandan: Sandalwood; Chandan, in the form of paste, is offered to Gods during worship

Chandran: Moon; radiant

Chandrashekhar: One who holds the moon at his peak; derived from the combination of two words, 'chandra' and 'shekhar' meaning 'moon' and 'peak' respectively; another name for Lord Shiva, who holds the crescent moon in his hair knot

*Charan: Feet; support; it is a custom in the Hindu religion to touch the 'charan' of elders to receive their blessings

#Chetan: Perceptive; live

Chiman: Curious; inquisitive

Chinmay: Supreme consciousness; full of knowledge

Chintan: Process of thinking; meditation

*#Chirag: Lamp; ray of hope

Chiranjiv: Immortal; longlived

D

Daksh: Capable; able; son of Lord Brahma

Dakshesh: Talented; perfect; another name for Lord Shiva

Daman: Controller; over-powering

Damodar: One with a rope around his waist; another name for Lord Krishna

Danvir: Charitable, one who donates generously

Darpak: Pride; another name for Kamdev, God of love

Darpan: Mirror; one who is self-reflective

Darsh: Worth looking at; another name for Lord Krishna

*Darshan: Paying respect; vision; to see

Dayanand: Merciful; sympathetic

Debashish: Blessings of God

Debjit: One who has conquered Gods

*Deepak/Deep: Light; lamp; that which illuminates

*Dev: Divinity; a class of Gods; a title of honour

Devaj/Devang: From God; derived from the word 'dev' meaning 'God'

*Deven/Devendra/Devesh: Chief of Gods; another name for Lord Indra

Devraj: King of Gods; derived from the words 'dev' and 'raj' meaning 'God' and 'king' respectively

Dhananjay: One who wins wealth; from the words 'dhan' meaning 'wealth' and 'jay' meaning 'victory'; another name for Arjuna

Dhanraj: King of wealth; derived from the words 'dhan' meaning 'wealth' and 'raj' meaning 'king'

Dharmesh: Lord of righteousness; lord of religion; 'dharma' means 'religion'

Dheeman/Dhimant: Intelligent; wise; learned

#Dheeraj/Dhiraj: Patience; tolerence

*#Dhiren: Strong

*Dhruv: Firm; constant; permanent; polar star

Dilip: Protector; caretaker; generous

Dinesh: The sun

Dipen/Dipesh: Flame of a lamp; one who enlightens; Lord of the light

#Divit: Immortal; long lived

Divyesh: Full of divinity; religious

Drupad: Determined; quick-footed; the word is from 'druta pada', which means 'walk quickly and finish your duty'; a king; Drupad is the father of Draupadi in the mythological epic Mahabharata

Dushyant: One who eradicates evil

Dyumna: Glorious; splendour; one who controls with divine powers

E

*Eashan/Eshaan: Wish; desire; another name for Lord Vishnu

Ehimay: An omnipresent intellect

Ekansh: Whole; one; from the word 'eka' meaning 'one'

Ekaraj: The sole emperor; the only king; derived by combining 'eka' and 'raj' meaning 'one' and 'king' respectively

Ekavir: Bravest

Eklavya: One with depth of knowledge; according to the Indian myth Mahabharata, Eklavya built a statue of Guru Dronacharya to inspire him as he taught himself to shoot a bow and arrow

Etash: Luminous; bright; shining

Evyavan: Possessed with speed; one who is swift; another name for Lord Vishnu

F

Falak: Heaven; sky

Falgun: Name of a Hindu month

Fanish: Another name for the mythical cosmic snake, Shesh Naag (a cobra)

G

*Gagan: Sky; heaven

Ganak: Astrologer; an expert in calculation and maths

Gandharv: Master in music; musician who entertains God

Gandhik: Fragrance; aroma; derived from the word 'gandh' meaning 'fragrant'

Ganesh: The God Ganesh has the face of an elephant. It is believed that worshipping Ganesh at the beginning of an event ensures that it will run smoothly and without complication. Ganesh was the son of Lord Shiva and Goddess Parvati

Gatik: Fast; progressive; derived from the word 'gati' meaning 'speed'

Gaurang: Melody; fair complexioned

*#Gaurav: Prestige; honour; respect; glory

Gautam: The enlightened one; another name for Lord Buddha

Geet: Melody; song

Ghanshyam: The dark complexioned one; one of the names of Lord Krishna

Giri: Mountain

Giridhar: One who lifts the mountain; one of the names of Lord Krishna, referring to the story where Lord Krishna held a mountain on his little finger; derived from combining two words, 'giri' which means 'mountain' and 'dhar' which means 'to hold', thus meaning 'holder of the mountain'

Girik: One living on the mountain; another name for Lord Shiva who is believed to stay on the holy mountain of 'Kailash' in the Himalayan ranges

Giriraj/#Girish: God/King of the mountains, derived from the base word 'giri' meaning 'mountain'; another name for Lord Shiva

Gopal/*Govind/Govinda: One who tends cows; a cowherd; one of the names of Lord Krishna; Govinda is one of the greatest comedy actors of Bollywood

Goral: Lovable one; one who is liked by everybody

Grishm/Grishma: Heat; summer season

Gunamay/Gunvant: Virtuous; one with good qualities; derived from the word 'guna' meaning 'good qualities'

Gurudutt: Bestowed by the guru; given by the teacher

Gyan: Knowledge

H

Hakesh: King of sound; one with a good voice

Hanshal: Swan-like; derived from the word 'hansa' meaning 'swan'

Hansraj: King of swans; derived from the combination of two words, 'hansa' meaning 'swan' and 'raj' meaning 'king'

Hardik: Full of love; heartfelt

*Haresh/#Harish: Lord Shiva and Lord Vishnu

Harij: The horizon, the imaginary line where the earth meets the sky

Harith: The colour green

*Harsh: Joy; happiness

Harshad/Harshit/Harsith/Hasit: Happy; one who showers joy; joyful

Harshul: Cheerful; joyful; another name for Lord Buddha

Hasan: Laughter

Hasmukh: Always smiling; derived by combining two words 'hasa' and 'mukha' meaning 'smile' and 'face' respectively, thus meaning one with a smile on his face

Havish: The sacrificing one; another name for Lord Shiva

Hemal: Golden

Hemang: One with a golden body; another name for Lord Vishnu

#Hemant: Winter; cold

Hemen: King of gold

Hemish: Lord of the earth

Himanish: One who lives in 'hima' (snow); another name for Lord Shiva, who is believed to live in the Himalayas (mountains of snow)

Himanshu: Moon; someone who is soft and pleasant

Himmat: Brave; courageous

Hiranmay: Full of gold; golden; precious

#Hiren: One possessing the qualities of gems and pearls, from the base word 'hira' meaning 'gem'

Hiresh: King of precious stones

*Hiten/Hitendra/Hitesh: Well-wisher; derived from the base word 'hita' meaning 'welfare'

Hrishikesh: One who has control over himself; one who has control over his senses; another name for Lord Vishnu

Hritik/Hrithik: Purity of the soul attained by those who perform Havan, a form of worship; a spiritual connotation; name of a sage

Hrydai: Heart; soul

I

Idhant: Luminous; one who spreads light

Ikshan: Vision; sight

Inas: Capable; strong; powerful

Indivar: The blue lotus; blessings; another name for Lord Vishnu

Indrajit: 'Jit' means 'victory', thus Indrajit means victory over Indra; the greatest conqueror

Indrasen: Lord Indra's army; derived from the word 'sena' meaning 'army'; Indrasen is the charioteer of Yudhisthira, the eldest of the Pandavas in the Indian myth, Mahabharata

Inesh: King; another name for Lord Vishnu

Inoday: Sunrise; from the word 'uday' which means 'to rise'

Iraj: Pertaining to the wind; another name for Lord Hanuman who is the son of God Vayu (wind God) in the Indian mythological epic Ramayana

Iravan: King of the ocean; possessing water in abundance

Iravat: Rain clouds; clouds full of water

*Ishaan: Sun; fire; one with the glory and power of the sun; another name for Lord Shiva

Ishan: Lord of wealth

Ishat: Superior; one who has the upper hand

Ishayu: One who is full of strength and power

Ishit: One who desires to rule

J

Jagat: World; universe

Jagdeep: Light of the universe; derived from 'jaga' and 'deep' meaning 'world' and 'light' respectively

Jagdish: King of the world

Jagrav: Awakened; watchful; alert

Jaideep: Light/glow of victory

Jaidev/Jairaj: King of victory; champion

Jaiman: Victorious; successful

Jaisukh: Happiness of the victory

Jaivant: Victory over life; longlived

Jaldhar: Clouds; derived from the words 'jala' meaning 'water' and 'dhar' meaning 'to hold', thus Jaldhar means 'one who holds water', i.e. cloud

Jalesh: Lord of water, derived from 'jala' meaning 'water'

Janak: From the word 'janan' which means 'to generate' or 'to give birth', thus Janak means father; one who has knowledge and is intelligent; another name for Lord Buddha; Janak was the father of Sita in the Indian mythological epic Ramayana

Janesh: King of men, derived from 'jana' meaning 'population' or 'people'

Janmesh: One who shapes his own future; one who holds his future; the king of his kundali (kundali, also known as horoscope, is the birth chart according to Hindu Vedic astrology)

Jashith: Protector; guardian

Jatan: Nurturing; preserving

Jatin: Referring to a saint; one who has 'jata' (long hair); another name for Lord Shiva

Jawahar: Gem; jewel; precious stone

*Jay/Jai: Victory; another name for Lord Indra

Jayant: Victorious in the end; derived from two words, 'jaya' and 'anta', meaning 'victory' and 'end' respectively; another name for Lord Shiva

Jayendra/Jinendra/Jayesh: Lord of victory

Jayin: Conqueror

*Jeevan: Life

Jigar: Heart

Jignesh: Intellectual curiosity

Jinesh: Lord of victory (according to the Jain religion)

Jitendra: One who has control over his senses

Jugal: Couple; pair; being together

$\mathcal{K}$

Kailash: Name of a mountain in the Himalayan ranges; abode of Lord Shiva

Kairav: White lotus; born in the water

Kallol: Shout of joy; surge of happiness

Kalpak: One of a certain quality; a heavenly tree, a tree in Lord Shiva's garden

Kalpesh: One who is perfect; one who seeks perfection

Kalyan: Good fortune; welfare; beneficial

*Kamal: Lotus; radiant like a lotus

Kamesh: Lord of love; one who showers love on everyone

Kamlesh: The preserver; God of lotus, Lord Brahma

Kamod: One who fulfils wishes; a Raga

Kamran: Success

Kanak: Gold; precious; sandalwood tree

Kanan: Forest

Kanav: Talented; intelligent; clever; a Hindu sage

Kanishk: Name of a king who was a follower of Buddhism

Kanj: Born from water; lotus; another name for Lord Brahma

Kapil: Sun; tanned complexion; a sage on whose preachings the Yoga science was developed; Kapil Dev is one of the greatest Indian cricketers of all time, who held the record for the highest number of wickets in test cricket

Kapish: King of the monkeys; another name for Lord Hanuman who was in the form of a monkey

*Karan/Karna: Ear; skilled; wise; an instrument; Karan was the son of the sun God and Kunti, and was born with a golden shield, according to the mythological epic Mahabharata

Kartik: Courageous; brave; a Hindu month; brother of Lord Ganesh and son of Shiva and Parvati

Karunesh: Lord of forgiveness and sympathy

Kashi: Luminous; shining; bright; most sacred Hindu pilgrimage spot in India

Kashish: Lord of Kashi; another name for Lord Shiva

Kaushal: Wealth; prosperity; welfare

Kaushik: One who knows hidden resources and assets; a wise sage

Kautik: Joy

*Kavi: A poet; a learned one; intelligent one

Kavin: Handsome; beautiful; a Tamil (south Indian/north Sri Lankan) name meaning 'natural beauty'

Kavish: King of poets; other name for Lord Ganesh in his persona as the God of poetry

Kedar: Pasture; grazing land; a Raga; the name of one of the mountains of the Himalayan ranges; another name for Lord Shiva

Keshav: One who has long or thick hair, from the word 'kesh' meaning 'hair'; another name for Lord Krishna

Ketak: Flower; ornament worn in the hair

*#Ketan: Home; house; banner; sign

Ketubh: Cloud

Khushal/*Kushal: Happy; skilled; efficient

*Kiran/Kiren: Sun rays/rays of light; minute particle

Kirin: One who praises by way of singing, writing or speaking; a poet; an author; a leader

Kirit: Crown; a symbol of pride

Kirti: Fame; glory; splendour; celebrity

*Kishan: Dark skinned; another name for Lord Krishna

Kishor/Kishore: Youngster; adolescent; teenager; another name for the sun God

Koshin: A delicate bud; mango tree

Kovidh: Wise; intelligent; clever

Kripal: Compassionate; kind; considerate

*Krishna: Dark skinned; one of the incarnations of Lord Vishnu, Lord Krishna

Krishi: Cultivating; the earth

*Krishnan: The centre of the eye (pupil); black

Krupal: Kind-hearted; generous

Kshitij: The horizon; the imaginary line where the earth or ocean meets the sky

*Kunal: Lotus; a bird; Kunal was the son of the great King Ashoka, named after his birdlike eyes

*#Kush: A type of holy grass used to worship deities during sacred ceremonies; twin son of Lord Rama and Sita

Kushad: Talented; one with a sharp mind

L

Labh: Gain; profit

Lahar: Wave

Lakhan/Laxman: One who accomplishes his goal; Lord Rama's half brother in the Indian mythological epic Ramayana

Laksh/Lakshan: Aim; target; a hundred thousand

Lalan: Nurturing; fostering with care

Lalit: Of great beauty; pleasing; soft; gentle; fine

Larraj: A sage; wise; learned; knowledgeable

Lav/#Luv: Tiny particles; twin son of Lord Rama and Sita

Lekh: Document; manuscript

Lochan: Bright, beautiful eyes

Lokesh: King of all people; another name for Lord Brahma

Lomash: A sage; one covered with hair

M

Madan: Delightful; another name for Kamdev, the God of love

Madhav: Sweet like honey; God of spring; another name for Lord Krishna

Madhuk: Honey bee; one who makes honey

Magan: Absorbed; engrossed; occupied

Mahavir: The most courageous one; the bravest of all; the last of the 24 Tirthankars (Gods) of the present Avasarpini of the Jain religion

Mahendra: King of all Gods; another name for Lord Vishnu

#Mahesh: Supreme God; another name for Lord Shiva

*Mahin: The earth; one that gives joy

*Mahir: Expert; skilled; productive

Mahit: Honoured; privileged; respected; a three pronged spear belonging to Lord Shiva

Maitreya: Friendly; pleasant

Makrand: Honey; nectar; sweet

Makul: Bud; young; adolescent

Malank: A king

Malhar: One who brings rain; one of the musical Ragas

Manas: A thought; originating in the mind; visualisation

*Manav: Man

Mandar: A divine tree; a determined person

Mangal: Auspicious; lucky; fortunate; Hindu name for the planet Mars

Mangesh: The Kuladevata (family deity) of millions of Hindus around the world; another name for Lord Shiva

Manik: Ruby; a precious stone, gem; respected

Manish: King of the mind; a wise person; derived from the word 'maan' which means 'mind'

Manit: Highly respected; esteemed

Mannan: Thought

Manohar: One who wins hearts and minds; another name for Lord Krishna

Manoj: Born with intelligence

Mansukh: Pleasing; enjoyable; lovely

Maulik: Precious; valuable; dear

#Mayank: Moon; spotted like a deer

#Mayur: Peacock; elegant

Medhansh: Born with intelligence

Meer: Chief; head; foremost

Meet: Friend; companion

Meghaj: Pearl; water; born from clouds; from the word 'megha' meaning 'cloud'

Mehal: Clouds

*Mehul: Rain

*Mihir: Sun; one that gives light and heat; a sage

Milan: Meeting; coming together

Miland/Milind: One looking to meet; bee

Milit: Camaraderie; friendship

Miten: Male friend

Mithun: A pair; the Hindu name for the zodiac sign of Gemini

Mitrajit: Friendly; one who has many friends; derived from the words 'mitra' and 'jeet' meaning 'friend' and 'winning' respectively

Mittul/Mitul: Measured; calculated; precise

Modak: Pleasing; agreeable; enjoyable

*Mohan: Lovable; charming; fascinating; another name for Lord Krishna

#Mohit: Enchanted by beauty; smitten with love; obsessed

Mohnish: Attractive one; another name for Lord Krishna

Mrigaj: Born of the moon

Mrigank: Moon; one marked like a deer; derived from the word 'mriga' meaning 'deer'

Mrigesh: Lion; king of the beasts

Mudil: Moonlight

Mudit: Happy; glad; derived from the word 'muda' meaning 'happiness'

#Mukesh: Lord of joy; Lord of freedom; another name for Lord Shiva

Mukul: Soul; hidden; bud

Mukund: Precious jewel; valuable stone; one who gives freedom; another name for Lord Krishna

Munish: Chief of sages; a Buddha

N

Nachiket: Fire; unaware; an ancient sage

Nadish: Ocean; Lord of water

Nagesh: King of snakes; derived from the word 'naga' meaning 'snake', thus 'nagesh' meaning 'Lord/king of snakes'; another name for Lord Shiva, as Shiva has a snake around his neck

Nairit: South west

Nakul: A musical instrument; one of the 5 Pandav princes; another name for Lord Shiva

Nalesh: King of flowers

Nalin: Lotus; one born in water

Naman: Renowned; famous; well known; salutation; offering prayer to God and elders

Namish: Well known; famous; another name for Lord Vishnu

Nandan: Son; enjoying; happy

Nandish: One who enjoys; king of happiness; another name for Lord Shiva

*Narayan: One who protects mankind; one of the incarnations of Lord Vishnu

#Narendra/#Naresh: King of men; superior; derived from the word 'nara' meaning 'man'

Narun: Leader of mankind

Natesh: King of dancers, the best dancer; derived from the word 'nata' which means 'dancer'; another name for Lord Shiva who is considered to be a good dancer

Nathan: The protector, defender; one who guards; another name for Lord Krishna

Navaj: Newly born, from the word 'nava' which means 'new'

Navashen: One who brings hope

*Naveen/Navin: New; recent; original

*Navrang: Colourful; one with a lively personality; derived from the words 'nava' meaning 'new' and 'ranga' meaning 'colours'

Navtej: New vigour, derived from 'nav' meaning 'new' and 'tej' meaning 'vigour'

*Nayan: Eye; head; chief; one who guides

*Neel/Neil: Blue; sapphire; mountain

Neeraf: River

*#Neeraj/Niraj: Born in water; radiant; one who is free from bad habits

Nibodh: One who possesses wisdom; intelligent

Nihal: Content; gratified; pleased

Nihar: Mist; fog; dew

Nikash: Horizon; benchmark; appearance

Niket: Home; residence

*#Nikhil: Complete; whole; entire

Nikunj: Grove of trees; garden; home; residence

Nilabh: Of blue colour; bluish shade; another name for the moon

Nilay: Haven; house

Nilesh: The blue Lord; another name for Lord Krishna; another name for the moon

Nimay: Adjusting; another name for the sage Chaitanya

Nimish: Momentary; very fast; another name for Lord Vishnu

Ninad: Humming; sound

Nipun: Expert; proficient; skilful

Nirad: Cloud; one that gives water to all

Niranjan: One without any marks; clean; pure; another name for Lord Shiva

Nirav: Silent; calm

Nirbhay/Nirbhik: Fearless, derived from 'bhay' meaning 'fear', 'nir' negates the meaning, thus meaning without fear

Nirek: Superior; better; higher

Nirmal/Nirmay: Clean; pure; hygienic

Nirmit: Created; formed; produced

Nischal: Firm; resolved; steady; immovable

Nishant: End of the night; end of the dark; early morning; dawn; peaceful; derived from the combination of 'nisha' meaning 'night' and 'anta' meaning 'end'

Nishesh: Lord of the night; moon

Nishith: Born at night

#Nishok: One who is happy, content; derived from the word 'shok' meaning 'sorrow', 'ni' creates its antonym, thus meaning without sorrow

#Nitin: One who has knowledge of law; one who lays down the guiding principles; from the base word 'niti' meaning 'policy'

Nitish: Master of law

O

Ojas: Vitality; energy; strength

Ojayit: One who is courageous; brave; bold

Om: Primordial sound; sacred syllable used for Hindu prayer

***Omkar/Onkar**: A prayer using the sacred syllable 'Om'

Omprakash: The sacred light spread by the syllable 'Om'; derived from the words 'om' meaning 'sacred' and 'prakash' meaning 'light'

P

Padmaj: Born from a lotus; derived from the word 'padma' meaning 'lotus'; another name for Lord Brahma

Padmesh: King of the lotus; another name for Lord Vishnu

Palash: Leaves shed by a tree; the foliage of a tree

Palin: Protect; defend; take care of

Panav: Prince; young; small

Pankaj: Lotus; born in the mud; another name for Lord Brahma

#Parag: The pollen grains of a flower

Paras: A magical stone that turns metal to gold by touch

Paresh: Supreme spirit; another name for Lord Brahma

Parikshit: Proven; fully tested; another name for earth

Parimal: Fragrance; aroma; scent

Paritosh: Delight; joy; happiness

***Parth**: King; another name for Arjun

Parthiv: Prince of earth; from the word 'prithvi' meaning 'earth'

Parvesh: Lord of celebration

*Pavan/Pawan: Sacred; pure; holy; wind; breeze

Pinak: A bow; bow of Lord Shiva

#Piyush: Amrit (divine drink); nectar; drink that makes one immortal

Prabal: Strong; physically powerful; well-built

Prabhakar: One who spreads light to all; another name for the sun

Prabhat: Dawn; morning

Prabodh: Consciousness; awareness; understanding

Prachet: Intelligent; clever; another name for Lord Varun

#Pradeep: Lamp; light; illuminating

Pradyumna: Very strong; muscular; another name for Kamdev, God of love

Pradyun: Radiant; joyful; healthy

Prafull: Playful; in bloom

Prahlad: Bliss; delight; happiness

Prajesh: King of living creatures; another name for Lord Brahma

Prajit: Winning; conquering

#Prakash: Light; brightness; sunshine

Praket: Intelligence; wisdom; knowledge

Prakhar: Sharp minded; keen

Prakrit: Pertaining to nature

Prakul: Good looking; handsome

#Pramod: Joy; gladness; happiness

Pran: Life; force

Pranad: Giving life; from the word 'pran' which means 'life'; another name for Lord Vishnu and Lord Brahma

*Pranav: A prayer using the sacred syllable 'Om'

Pranay: Love; affection; leader; chief

Prasad: Devotional offering; food offered to God during puja

*Prashant: Cool; calm; composed; peaceful

Pratap: Bravery; heroism; courageous act

*Pratham/Prathamesh: First; Lord of the best; another name for Lord Ganesh

Pratik: Symbol; image

*Pravin/Praveen: Expert; experienced; skilled

Pratyus: Before morning; dawn

*Prem/Prit: Love; affection

Prineet: Content; satisfied; pleased; delighted

Pritam: Beloved; darling; loved one, from the word 'prit' which means 'love'

Pritesh: Lord of love

Prithvi/Pruthvi: Earth; world; globe

Punit/Puneet: Pure; holy; sacred

R

Rachit: To create; to generate; to produce

Radhesh: Lord of Radha; another name for Krishna

Raghav: Born in the Raghu family; another name for Lord Rama

Raghuveer: Brave man of the Raghu family; derived by combining two words 'raghu' and 'veer' meaning 'of the raghu family' and 'brave' respectively; another name for Lord Rama

*Rahul: Capable; efficient; son of Lord Buddha

*Raj: Kingdom

*Raja/Rajan: King; ruler; belonging to the royal family

Rajat: Silver; bright

Rajdeep: Lamp among the kings; best among the kings

Rajeev/Rajiv: Striped; a kind of fish; of the lotus; Rajiv Gandhi was the youngest prime minister of India

#Rajesh/Rajendra: King of kings; the greatest king

Rajanish: Lord of the night; moon; derived from the word 'rajani' meaning 'night'

#Raju: King; sovereign

#Rakesh: Lord of the full moon; derived from the word 'raka' which means 'the day of the full moon'; another name for Lord Shiva

Raman: Pleasing; charming; charismatic; beloved; another name for Kamdev, God of love

Ramesh: The preserver; another name for Lord Vishnu

Ranak: King; fighter

Randhir: A warrior who shows bravery, control and patience during war; derived from the words 'rana' meaning battleground and 'dhir' meaning patience

Ranjit: Victor in war; derived from the combination of two words, 'rana' and 'jit' meaning 'battleground' and 'victory' respectively

Rasik: Elegant; tasteful; humorous; enthusiastic

Ratan: Gem; precious stone; jewel

Ratish/Renesh: Alternative names for Kamdev, God of love

*Ravi/Ravit: Sun; fire

Rishabh: Superior; best; morality; the second note in an octave; the first of the twenty-four 'Tirthankars' (Gods) of the Jain religion

*Rishi: A sage; ray of light; one who sings sacred hymns

Rishit: The best; the top; the greatest

#Ritesh: Lord of truth; honest

Rithik: Stream

*Rohan: Ascending; developing bud; another name for Lord Vishnu

*#Rohit: Sun; red

*Ronak: Celebration; embellishment; decoration

*Ronit: Song; tune; chant

*Roshan: Illumination; passionate; loving

Ruchir: Radiant; bright; handsome; good-looking

Rupesh: Lord of beauty, from the word 'rupa' meaning 'beauty'

*Rushil: Charming; polite; amiable

Rustom: Warrior

S

Sachet: Consciousness

*Sachin: Pure existence; affectionate; Sachin Tendulkar is a world-renowned Indian cricket player, also known as 'Wonder Boy' for his exceptional skills and the number of world records he has set; another name for Lord Shiva

Sachish: Lord of Sachi; Sachi in this context means kindness, favour; another name for Lord Indra

Sadashiv: Pure; 'shiva' means 'eternal goodness', always kind, happy and prosperous

Sadhil: Perfect; a master

*Sagar: Sea; ocean

Sahar: Sun; dawn

Saharsh: Glad; 'harsh' means 'joy', 'sa' at the front of the name means 'with', to mean 'with joy' or 'joyful'

Sahas: Bravery; courageous deed

Sai/Sainath: Another name for God; another name for Saint Saibaba who was from a village called Shirdi in the Maharashtra state of India

Sajiv: Lively; alive; 'jiva' means 'life', and 'sa' at the front of the name means 'with', meaning 'with life' or 'full of life'

Sakash: Illumination; shining light; Kashi is the most sacred place of pilgrimage in India, where the famous Vishvanath temple is located, whose Shivalinga (representation of Lord Shiva) is considered to have been installed by Lord Brahma. Hence Sakash is the one whose soul is shining with divine light

Saket: Another name for Lord Krishna; another name for the town of Ayodhya

Salil: Water; that which is flowing

Samarth: A smooth chariot; the name of the brother of King Varat who supported Pandavas in Mahabharat; since Saint Ramadas had the extraordinary capacity to do many great things, he came to be known as Samarth Ramadas, the appellation Samarth meaning a man of versatile skills; another name for Lord Krishna

Sameep: Closeness; proximity

*Sameer/Samir: The fresh smell of morning; entertaining companion; breeze

Samrudh: The enriched one

Sanchay: Collection

*#Sandeep: Glowing; Rishi (Sage of Gods), named after Sandipani Rishi. Krishna and Balarama learnt all the skills and scriptures from Sandipani Rishi in just sixty-four days

Sandesh: Message

*Sanjay: Victorious; triumphant; according to Mahabharata, Sanjay was a minister of King Dhritarashtra. He was blessed with divine sight, and was able to see the battle between the Pandavas and Kauravas without physically being at the battlefield

Sanjiv: Vital; possessed with life; living

Sanket: Signal; sign; indication

Santosh: Satisfaction; Tushita, son of Dharma and Tushi, is supposed to be the representation of satisfaction (Santosh)

Sarang: Dappled; spotted; a musical instrument; a spotted antelope; name of a Raga; another name for Lord Shiva

Saransh: Summary; brief; precise; concise

Saras: The moon; coming from the lake

Sashang: Associated; connected

Satin: Real; essential; truth; derived from the word 'sati' meaning 'truthful'; 'sati' is the act of a widow immolating herself on her husband's funeral pyre

Satish: Lord of Sati (see Satin); another name for Lord Shiva

Satvik: Virtuous; derived from the word 'satva' meaning 'true essence'; life

Satyajit: Victory of truth; formed from 'satya' and 'jit' meaning 'truth' and 'victory' respectively

Satyam: Truthfulness; honesty

Saumit/Saumitra: Easy to get; derived from the word 'saumya' meaning 'mild' or 'gentle'; Saumitra is another name for Lakshmana, Lord Rama's brother in the Indian mythological story, Ramayana

Saurabh: Fragrant; perfumed

#Saurav: Melodious; harmonious

*Shaan: Pride

Shaarav: Innocent; pure

Shailesh/Shailendra: Lord of the mountain

Shakti: Power; strength; energy; the power of the Lord which is expressed in the workings of prakruti (nature)

Shamak: The one who makes peace; pacifier; derived from 'shama' meaning 'peace'

Shanay: The power of Lord Shani

Shantanu: Whole; complete; Shantanu is the father of Bhishma, according to the mythological epic, Mahabharata

Sharad: Autumn; name of a season

Shardul: Tiger; best; reputed; according to the Indian mythological epic Ramayana, Shardul was Ravana's spy

Shashank: The moon

Shaunak: Wise; Shaunak was a famous grammarian and teacher

Shekhar: Ultimate; peak; best; chief

Shishir: Winter; cold; frost

Shishul: Baby; toddler; little one

*Shivam/Shiv: Auspicious/prosperous; Lord Shiva is a God with three eyes, with the middle one in his forehead which holds the crescent moon. His coiled hair bears the River Ganga, and he has snakes around his neck

*Shreyas: The best; most handsome; luckiest

Shridhar/Shrikant: Referring to 'shri', the holy one; another name for Lord Vishnu

Shubha: Fortunate; auspicious; lucky

Shubhay: Blessing; to wish 'shubha' (good fortune) on somebody

*Shyam: One with a dark complexion; night; another name for Lord Krishna

Siddhant: Moral; ethical; one who has strong principles of life

Siddharth: The accomplished one; Prince Siddharth was renamed Buddha (meaning 'enlightened one') after he wandered from place to place, preaching his message

Siddhesh: Lord of 'Siddha'; the perfect one; the complete one

*Sivakumar: Son of Lord Shiva; derived from the combination of two words 'Shiva' (Lord Shiva) and 'kumar' (son)

Sohan: Handsome; charming

Sourabh: Fragrance; smell

Sparsh: Touch

Stavya: One who is admirable; God

Subhash: One who speaks good words; from the Sanskrit word 'bhashya' meaning 'commentary', 'su' at the front of the word means 'good'

Subodh: Excellent teaching; fine intellect

Suchet: One with a good soul; attentive; alert

Suchit: Person with a sound mind, one who does not get distracted by temptations; another name for Lord Bramha who also symbolises purity of the soul; from 'chit' meaning 'mind', 'su' at the beginning of the word gives the meaning 'good mind'

Suday: Auspicious gift

Sudeep: Bright; brilliant; radiant

Sudhanshu: The moon; camphor

Sudhir: Wise; firm; determined; great scholar

Suhas: Laughter; one with a stunning smile

Sujay: Huge victory; immense success

Sujit: Victory; good conquest; 'jita' means 'victory' and the preceding 'su' gives the meaning 'good victory'

***Sukhesh/Sukhraj**: Lord of happiness; derived from the word 'sukha' meaning 'happiness'

Sukumara: Very tender; very delicate; another name for Champaka, a delicate flower

#Sumant: A king's minister; intelligent person; friendly

Sumedh: Clever; intelligent

Sumeet/#Sumit: A good friend; well balanced

Sunay: Wise; a well-conducted person; best path of life

***#Sunil/Suneel**: Blue; sapphire; pomegranate tree; another name for Lord Krishna

***Sunny**: Brightness of the sun; shiny; Sunny Deol is a well-known Bollywood actor

***Suraj**: The sun; one who illuminates mind and soul

#Surendra: King of Suras, 'Sura' meaning 'God'; another name for Lord Indra

#Suresh: God of Suras; another name for Lord Shiva and Lord Indra

Sushant: Quiet; calm; peaceful person

Sushil: Good charactered; well mannered; virtuous

Swajit: Own victory; formed by the combination of 'swayam' meaning 'myself' and 'jit' meaning 'victory'

Swapnil: Dreamy; derived from the word 'swapna' meaning 'dream'

Swastik: Auspicious; fortunate; a religious symbol

T

Tanay: Of the family; son

Tanish: Ambition; aim; goal

Tanishq: Valuable; precious; diamond

Tanmay: Reincarnated; concentrate; engrossed; absorbed

Taraksh: Mountain; radiant eyed

*Taran: Heaven; thunder; earth; another name for Lord Vishnu

Tarang: Wave

*#Tarun: Youth; tender

Tavish: Heaven; gold; energetic; lively; active

*Tej/Tejas: Light; effulgence; light of energy; Tejas is one of the five 'Bhutas' – the external, unchanging matrix of elements which comprises aakash (sky), vayu (air), agni/tejas (fire), apas/jala (water) and prithvi (earth)

Toyesh: Lord of water, from the word 'toya' meaning 'water'

Turag: A thought; one that moves swiftly, represented by the white horse that emerged as a result of Samudra Manthanam (ocean churning) in Mahabharata

Tushar: Fine drops of water; dew; mist

$\mathcal{U}$

Uchit: Correct; proper

Udant: Correct message

Udarsh: Brimming; overflowing; full

Uday: Sunrise; to rise; prosperity

Uddhav: Festival; sacrificial yagna (fire); name of Lord Krishna's friend

Udit: Arisen; shining; awakened; Udit Narayan is one of India's renowned singers

Ulhas: Joy; happiness; delight

Umakant/Umesh: Lord of the night or moonlight, derived from the word 'uma' meaning 'night' or 'moonlight'; another name for Lord Shiva

Unmesh: Blossoming of a flower; flashing; revelation

Upendra: Younger to Indra – Upendra was born to Adhithi Devi as a younger son after Indra was born; another name for Lord Vishnu

Urvang: Mountain; ocean; one who has huge body

Urvish: Lord of the earth

Utkarsh: High quality; prosperity; progression; evolution

Utpal: Burst open; blue lotus

V

Vaibhav: Glory; power; prosperity; riches

Vairaj: Spiritual glory

Vallabh: Most loved; dear; favourite

Valmiki: A white ant hill; 'Valmiki' became a name when some-one meditated for so long in one position that an anthill was built over his body; the name of the saint who wrote the Indian mythological epic, Ramayana

Vanad: Rain giving; cloud; derived from the word 'vana' which means 'forest that brings rain'

Vansh: Generation to come; son

Varad: God of fire; one who grants wishes; 'Varad' is a Hindu tradition of worshipping fire to have one's wishes granted

Varin: Gifts

*#Varun: Lord of water; wind; air; according to the Jain religion, 'Varun' is the servant of the 20th Arhat of the present Avasarpini

Vasant: Season; spring

Vasur: Precious; valuable

Vatsal: Love and affection towards children

Vayun: Lively; active

Vedang: A part of the Vedas, one of six sciences auxiliary to the Veda – chanting, ritual, grammar, vocabulary, speech interpretation (prosody), astrology

Vedant: Absolute truth; end or culmination of Vedas; Hindu philosophy

Venkat/Venkatesh: Self-born; divine; another name for Lord Vishnu and Lord Krishna

Vibhor: Ecstatic; overjoyed; thrilled

Vibhuti: Strong; powerful; ash which is auspicious and applied to the forehead for self-protection

Vibodh: Wise; intelligent; one with heightened perception

Vidip: Bright; light; clear

Vidur: Wise; Vidur was the uncle of Pandavas in Mahabharata (the Indian myth); also the name of the wisest minister in King Dhrutarashtra's cabinet in Mahabharata

Vidyut: Brilliant; lightning; electricity

Vignesh/Vighnesh: Removal of obstacles; another name for Lord Ganesh who is believed to remove all obstacles and is worshipped at the beginning of ceremonies

*#Vijay: Victory; success; triumph

Vikas: Progress; development

*Vikram: Brave; hero; praiseworthy act; record; another name for Lord Shiva

Vikrant: Brave; powerful

Vilas: Relaxation; leisure

Vimal: Clean; pure; Vimal is the thirteenth Tirthankara (God) of the Jain religion

*Vinay: Modesty; humility; the discipline practised by Buddhist monks

Vinayak: Leader; derived from the word 'nayak' which means 'leader', Vinayak means the one who has all the qualities of a leader; another name for Lord Ganesh

*Vinesh: Godly; religious; pious

#Vinit/Vineet: Polite; modest, unassuming; knowledgeable

#Vinod: Pleasant; happy; full of joy

#Vipin: Forest; woods

Vipul: Abundant; plentiful; large

Vir/Veer: Brave; hero

*Viraj: Sun; resplendent; dazzling; splendour; magnificence

Viral: Precious; priceless; dear

Virendra: Lord of the braves, derived from combining two words, 'vir' meaning 'brave' and 'indra' meaning 'Lord'

Viresh: Lord of the braves; another name for Lord Shiva

*#Vishal: Huge; big; immense; massive

Vishvajit: Conqueror of the world, from the combination of 'vishva' and 'jit' meaning 'world' and 'victory' respectively

Vishvas: Faith; trust; confidence

Vittesh: Lord of wealth; owner of money; another name for Lord Kuber

*Vivek: Intellect; discrimination between good and bad; judgment; true knowledge

Vyas: Distinction; separation; compiler; the name of the sage who wrote the Indian myth Mahabharata

Vyoman: Sky; heaven; wind

$\mathcal{Y}$

Yadav: One descended from a Yadu (cowherd's) family; a surname; another name for Lord Krishna, as his father 'Vasudev' was a cowherd

Yajat: Holy; divine; power of sacrifice; master of sacrifice; another name for Lord Shiva

*Yash: Success; victory; glory; fame; goodwill

Yashpal: Successful; famous; Lord of glory; protector of fame; derived from the word 'yash' meaning 'fame' or 'glory'

Yatin: Devotee; disciple; follower

Yodhin: Conqueror; warrior

#Yogesh: The master of Yoga; another name for Lord Shiva

Yuval: Brook; stream; rivulet

*Yuvraj: Prince; heir; young king; derived from the words 'yuva' and 'raj' meaning 'young' and 'king' respectively

Hindu Girls' Names

A

Aadita: Beginning; roots

Aahna: Immortal; eternal; never-ending

*Aaina: Mirror; one who has self-realisation; reflective one

Aakansha: Wish; desire; expectation

Aanchal: The decorative end of a saree (pallu); shelter; care

Aarini: Courageous; brave; daring; bold

Aarohi: Ascending; 'arohi' is a term from Indian classical music that means 'ascending melody'

Aarti/Arti: This is a form of worship where hymns are sung in praise of God while singers hold a lamp fuelled with oil or ghee. This divine service is usually performed in the early morning, or at dusk

*Aarushi: First rays; dawn; energy; enlightening

Aatmaja: Daughter; another name for Parvati, Lord Shiva's wife

Aayushi: One who will have a long life, derived from the word 'ayush' meaning 'duration of life'

Aboli: Name of a delicate flower

Achala: Constant; steady; immovable; mountain; earth; according to Jain beliefs, 'achala' is one of the nine Baladevas (Balabhadras)

*Aditi: Mother of Gods; supreme nature; infinity; mother of 'Aditya'; another name for earth

Advika: Unique; exclusive; only one of its kind

Ahanti: Indestructible; eternal

Ahilya: Sacred; Ahilya bai Holkar (1730–95) was one of India's celebrated female rulers

Aishi: Life; God's gift

*Aishwarya: Wealth; prosperity; one of the 'Ashta-siddhis' – the control over events or objects without physical aid; Aishwarya Rai was crowned Miss World 1994, and is one of Bollywood's leading actresses

Akanksha: Wish; desire; ambition; hope

Akshadha/Akshata: Holy rice grain; unbroken decorated rice. Traditionally, at Hindu weddings, everyone blesses the couple by showering them with 'akshadha' (decorated grains of rice); it is a custom to offer 'akshata' (whole rice-grain) to deities during worship and rituals

Akshaya/#Akshita: Imperishable; immortal; eternal; Goddess of earth

Alka: Girl with curly hair; one with beautiful hair

Alpa: Small; little; tiny

Alpana: Decorative design on the floor (rangoli); beautiful; good-looking

#Amala: Clean; pure; spotless; unpolluted; Hindi name for tamarind; another name for Goddess Lakshmi

*Amaya: Limitless; infinite; never-ending; night rain

*#Ambika: Mother; protective; caring; another name for Goddess Parvati, a Goddess who defeated the devil

*Amie/Amee: Beloved; dear

*#Amisha: Frank; honest; truthful

Amishi: Pure; clean; untainted

*#Amrita/Amruta: Full of nectar; spiritual holy water, 'Amrit' is a drink reputed to make one immortal

Anagha: Without sin; innocent; faultless; a river

Anandi: Joyful; jubilant; one who gives happiness to others

*#Anita: A leader; graceful; polished; elegant

*#Anjali: Tribute; offering; devotion; the traditional action of folding both hands to shower offerings on God

#Anjana: Mountain; the name of the mother of Hanuman

#Anju: One who lives in the heart; beloved

#Ankita: Distinguished; empress; marked by the Lord; one with auspicious marks

Annapoorna/Annapurna: Goddess of harvests; one who is generous with food; Goddess Annapurna is the presiding deity of Kashi, the most sacred place in India; the Annapurna region (named for the Annapurna mountain range) is the most popular trekking area in Nepal

Anokhi: Different; incomparable; only one of its kind

Anshuka: Tender; delicate; lustrous; ray; derived from the word 'Anshu' meaning 'minute particle' or 'sunbeam'

Antara: Inner beauty; interior; soul; the second note in Hindustani classical music

#Anuja: Lovable younger sister

#Anupama: Unique; matchless; one without comparison or equal; name of an elephant in the Indian myth, Purana

Anupriya: Beloved; dear one; dearly loved

#Anuradha: Name of a star; 'Anuradha' is the 17th of the 27 Nakshatras which contain three stars in the body of Scorpio – the stars of Anuradha are depicted as a staff or a row of offerings to the Gods

#Anushka/Anoushka: A term of endearment; one who has no enemies; lightning

Anushree: Glorious; celebrated; good-looking; beautiful; another name for Goddess Lakshmi

Anvi/Anavi: One who is generous to people; kind

#Aparna: Without leaves; derived from the word 'parna' meaning full of leaves, the preceding 'a' negates the meaning, thus meaning without leaves; another name for Goddess Parvati

Apurva: Like never before; extraordinary; unusual; special

#Aradhana: Worship; prayer; 'Aradhana' was a famous Hindi movie (1969) starring Rajesh Khanna and Sharmila Tagore, with music by SD Burman

#Archana: Worship, prayer; respected; a thing of truth and beauty

Arpita: Dedicated; presented; surrendered

Aruna: Dawn; red; passionate; productive

*#Asha: Hope; expectation; aspiration

Ashwini: Quick, swift; derived from 'ashwa' meaning 'horse', the word represents the swiftness and speed of the horse; the first of the 27 Nakshatras – Ashwini Nakshatra falls in the Mesh, which is ruled by the aggressive and fiery planet Mars

#Asmita: Pride; self-esteem; self-respect

Atheeva: Ultimate; outstanding

*Atiya: Outshine; outperform

Avanti: Modest; humble; name of a historical, sacred city

B

Babita: One born in the first quarter of the day

Bageshri: Name of an Indian Raga

Bela: Flowering creeper; fragrant flower; time; seashore

Bhagyashri: Lucky; fortunate; another name for Goddess Lakshmi

Bhairavi: A melody in classical music; another name for Goddess Durga

Bhakti: Prayer; worship; divine devotion; 'bhakti' is the pure love and devotion to a deity which leads to salvation and Nirvana

Bharati: Speech; the vastness of knowledge and truth; virtuous; another name for Goddess Saraswati, the Goddess of learning; belonging to 'Bharat', the Hindi name for India

Bhavika: Well-mannered; virtuous; dutiful

Bhavini: Emotional; sensitive; beautiful; another name for Goddess Parvati

Bhavna: Feelings; sentiments; idea; thought; meditation

Bhuvi: Paradise; kingdom of God

Bijal/Bijli: Lightning; electricity; energy; brightness; enlightenment

Bina: Melodious; musical instrument; intelligence; knowledge

Bindu: Dot; point; tip; end; top; summit; pearl; drop

Binita: Modest; humble; down-to-earth

Bishakha: A star, celebrity; famous

#Brinda: Tulsi (basil plant); surrounded; another name for Radha

C

Chaavi: Reflection; image; pretty; radiance

*#Chaaya: Shadow; shade where travellers get rest; name of a Raga

Chaitali: Girl born in the month of Chaitra (Hindu calendar); one with a sharp memory

Chameli: Jasmine flower (creeper with sweet scented flower)

Champa: The fragrant white flower of the Champak tree. Incense sticks often carry the aroma of Champak, as many find it soothing

Chandani: Moonlight; star; silver; another name for Goddess Devi

Charulata: Beautiful creeper, derived from combining two words, 'charu' meaning 'beautiful' and 'lata' meaning 'creeper'

Chetana: Consciousness; wisdom; knowledge; understanding; power of intellect; alert

Chitra: Drawing; portrait; painting; beautiful; the 14th of the 27 Nakshatras, which represents brightness; the name of a river

Chitrali: A row of pictures, derived from the word 'chitra' meaning 'picture'

𝒟

Daksha: The power of judgment; the earth; another name for Goddess Parvati, wife of Lord Shiva

Dakshata: Skill; talent; alertness

Damini: Lightning

Darpana: Mirror; glass; vanity; self-realisation; reflective

Darshana: Observation; sight; vision; the self-revelation of the Deity to the devotee

Deepa/*Deeya: Light; lamp; candle; brightness

Deepshika: Flame of a lamp, derived from two words, 'deep' meaning 'lamp' and 'shika' meaning 'top', thus meaning 'the top of the lamp' (i.e. the flame)

Deepti/Dipti: Full of light; glow; shine; brightness; illumination

Devangi: Like a Goddess; derived from merging two words, 'dev' and 'angi' meaning 'God' and 'body' respectively, thus meaning 'body like a God'

*Devika: Minor Goddess; a river in the Himalayan region

Devki: Holy; famous; self-righteous; Lord Krishna's mother

Devyani: Like a Goddess; daughter of Lord Shiva

Dhanashree: A Raga; Goddess of wealth; endowed with wealth; derived from the word 'dhana' meaning 'wealth'

Dhriti/Dhruti/Dhruvi: Firm; determined; steady; resolute; endurance; persistant

Diksha: Initiation; launch; commencement

Dipali/Deepali: Row of lamps or lights, derived from the word 'Deepawali' which is the festival of lights

Dipika: Little light; small lamp; brightness, illumination; a Raagini used in Indian music

*Disha: Direction; side; region

*Divya: Divine power; heavenly; beautiful; brilliant

Divyanshi: Part of divine power; derived from two words 'divya' meaning 'divine power' and 'ansh' meaning 'particle' or 'part'

Drishti: Eyesight; perception; vision of the spiritual consciousness; vision of truth

Durva: Holy grass – traditionally this is offered to Lord Ganesha during Puja. 'Durva' is very durable and is a symbol of long life

$\mathcal{E}$

*Eesha: Purity; transparency; another name for Goddess Parvati

Eila/Ela: The earth; motherly; caring

Ekaja/Ekani: Only child; born alone; single daughter; derived from the word 'eka' meaning 'one'

Ekanta: Devoted; dedicated; faithful; loyal

Ekantika: Singly focused; persistent in achieving goals

Ekta: Unity; unanimity; in harmony

Elina: Intelligent; bright; sharp; able

*#Esha: Desire; want; aspiration; wish

$\mathcal{F}$

Falguni: Beautiful; day of the full moon; one born in the Hindu month of Falgun

Foolan/Fulan: Flowering; blossoming; 'Foolan devi' is the famous bandit queen of India

Fulki: Sparkle; glow; shine

Fulwati: One as delicate as a flower; derived from the word 'ful' meaning 'flower'

G

Gandhali: Sweet scent; pleasant odour; enjoyable aroma; perfume

Ganika: Jasmine flower; one who has social consciousness

Garima: Warmth; affection; prowess; one of the 8 siddhis of yoga science

*Gauri: Fair complexioned; gold; yellow; shining; another name for Goddess Parvati

Gautami: One who spreads light; wife of Gautam; another name for the river Godavari; another name for Goddess Durga

Gayatri: The sacred Vedic mantra for bringing the light of truth into all parts of the being. 'Gaya' means 'to reveal' and 'tri' refers to the three Vedas, thus 'Gayatri' is the revelation of the meaning of the three Vedas – the song of the Vedas gives the highest form of liberation. Also the name of a Goddess, 'ga' means 'to sing' and 'yatri' means 'protection', thus those who worship the Goddess Gayatri are protected

#Geeta/Gita: The Holy book of the Hindus, Gita deals with supreme wisdom and comes to us in the form of a poetic dialogue. It examines the theory of rebirth and the origin of the universe, the nature of human beings, the concept of God and the different philosophies concerning God, and also shows the path to perfection

Girija: Daughter of the mountain, derived from the word 'giri' meaning 'mountain'; another name for Goddess Parvati

#Gitanjali: Melodious tribute; offering of religious songs; collection of poems; derived from the word 'gita' meaning 'song'; Rabindranath Tagore was the first Indian ever to receive a Nobel Prize for Literature in recognition of his collection of poems, Geetanjali, in 1913

Gomti: A river in northern India; region rich in cows; derived from the word 'go' meaning 'cow'

Greeshma/Grishma: Summer season; warmth; affection, tenderness, love

Gulika: A pearl; gem; round in shape

Gunita: Virtuous; proficient; talented; capable; derived from the word 'guna' meaning 'virtues and attributes'

Gunnika: Garland; well woven; necklace

ℋ

Haimi: Golden (according to Hindu meaning)

Hamsini: One who rides a swan; another name for Goddess Saraswati

Hansika/Hansini/Hansa: Swan; pretty; beautiful

Harita: Green

#Harsha/Harshini: Joy; happiness; pleasure

Harshada: Giver of joy; one who brings happiness

Harshita: Full of joy; one with a beautiful smile

*Hema: Gold; celestial maiden; beautiful; gorgeous

Hemal: Golden

Hemangi: Golden bodied; golden coloured; derived from the combination of 'hema' and 'ang' meaning 'golden' and 'body' respectively

Hemlata: Golden flower; golden creeper; derived from the combination of 'hema' meaning 'golden' and 'lata' meaning 'creeper' or 'flower'

*Henna: Also known as Mehndi, Henna is applied to an Indian bride's hands and feet as a symbol of good luck in married life

Hetal: Friendly; responsive; sociable

Himaja: Born from snow; daughter of the snow; another name for Goddess Parvati; derived from the word 'hima' meaning 'snow'

*#Himani: Snow; fair like the snow; another name for Goddess Parvati

*Hira/Heera: Diamond; precious; another name for Goddess Lakshmi who is considered to be the Goddess of wealth

Hiral: Wealthy; shiny; possessor of diamonds

Hitaishi: Well-wisher, from the word 'hita' meaning 'welfare'

I

Idha: Insight; diligent; hard-working; intellectual

Idika: Deep insight, derived from 'idha'; another name for the earth

Iha/Ihita: Desire; want; wish; aspiration

Ijaya: Sacrifice; forfeit; award; endowment

Iksha: Sight; vision into the future

Ikshita: Visible; perceptible; who is seen

Ila: One representing true vision; one revealing vision in knowledge; teacher; earth; island

Imani: Trustworthy; faithful; honest; faith in own beliefs and abilities

*Indira: Bestower of wealth; prosperity; splendid; another name for Goddess Lakshmi, wife of the Hindu God Vishnu; Indira Gandhi (1917–1984) was the first female Prime Minister of India

Indu: Moon; soma (a divine drink); Vedic libation (set of ancient Hindu life rules); a Hindu person is governed by Indu (Vedic libation)

Induja: Moon's daughter; alternative name for the Narmada River in India

Indumati: Full moon; pleasant; soothing; daughter of Vidharba and wife of Aja

Iraja: Wind's daughter; daughter of the earth, derived from the word 'Ira' meaning 'wind' and 'earth'

Iravati: Name of a river; filled with water

*Isha: Female energy; life; one who protects; another name for Goddess Durga; God; derived from the word 'Ishwar' meaning 'God'

*Ishika: Paintbrush; implement used to write with

Ishita: Superior; mastery; perfect control over the powers of nature; one of the 8 Siddhis

Ishya: Spring season; fulfilling wishes

Iyla: Moonlight; cool; pleasant

J

Jagruti: Awareness; consciousness; awakening; vigilant

Jagvi/Jagavi: Worldly; mature; derived from the word 'jaga' meaning 'world'

Janani: Mother; caring; loving; mother of all; derived from the word 'jana' meaning 'all of mankind'

*Janhavi: Sinless; another name for the River Ganga; derived from the word 'jahnu' which means 'one who is devoid of any sins', the River Ganga is also called 'Janhavi' because bathing in its water is said to cleanse people from sin

Janisha: Knowledgeable; dispeller of ignorance

Janki: Daughter of King Janak; another name for Sita, wife of Lord Rama

Januja: Daughter; baby girl; female child

Janya: Life; birth; sacred thread ceremony; Janya Raga is composed from a parent scale by omitting notes from the scale, by introducing a zig-zag pattern or by adding alien notes that are not present in the original parent scale

Jarul: Flower queen; beautiful; good-looking

Jasmin/Jasmine: A beautiful flower from the olive family, this fragrantly flowered shrub produces different coloured flowers – yellow Jasmine represents grace and elegance, white Jasmine represents amiability and Spanish Jasmine represents sensuality; dreaming of this flower is an omen of success in romantic or personal affairs

Jasu: Clever; intelligent

*Jaya: Victory; one who is victorious; successful; another name for Goddess Parvati; Jaya Bachchan, wife of Amitabh Bachchan, is one of Bollywood's famous actresses

Jayanti: Something that ends with victory; another name for Goddess Durga; derived from combining two words 'jaya' and 'anta' meaning 'victory' and 'the end' respectively

Jayashree: Victorious woman; honour of victory; Goddess of success; a Raga in Indian classical music

Jigisha: Superior; aspiring for victory; desire to learn

Jigyasa: Curious; inquisitive

Joshika: Young maiden; young woman

Juhi: A white flower; a scented flower

*Jyoti: Natural light; flame; lamp; shining

Jyotsna: Moonlight; radiant; another name for Goddess Durga

$\mathcal{K}$

*Kaajal/Kajol: Black mascara or eyeliner used to beautify the eyes

Kairavi: Moonlight

Kajri: Black coloured; like a cloud; Kajri is one of the most popular and well-known forms of folk music sung in the monsoon season. Mirzapur in the state of Uttar Pradesh is considered to be the home of the Kajri

Kala: Art; a piece; a part; phase of the moon

Kalpana: Imagination; idea; Kalpana Chawla was the first Indian-born woman in space

Kalpita: Imaginary; the pre-existing compositions of the hardcore classical music are called 'Kalpita', literally meaning 'that which is taught'

Kalyani: Fortunate; blissful; prosperity; an auspicious woman; descending order of the musical notes; a Ragini

Kamal/#Kamala: Lotus; beautiful; wealthy; another name for Goddess Lakshmi, the Goddess of wealth

Kamana/Kamna: Wish; desire; passion

Kamini: Beautiful woman; full of desires; loving

Kamya: Capable; in pursuit of desire; acts performed to attain a desired object

Kanchan: Gold; wealth; shining

Kanchi: Waistband; a religious place in south India

Kani: Girl; daughter

Kanta: Beauty; glowing; radiant

*Kareena: Pure; witty; cute; dear

*Karishma/Krishma: Miracle; wonder; sensation; Karishma Kapoor is the first daughter of the famous Kapoor clan to enter into the film industry

Karuna: Merciful; kind-hearted; sympathetic; one who acts to diminish the suffering of others; Karuna reiki is one of the newly developed reiki techniques

Kashmira: One who belongs to Kashmir; one of the names of the Goddess Parvati

Kashvi: Shining; glowing; beautiful

Kashwini: Star; famous; celebrity

Kasturi: Scent; musk; fragrance

Kaushalya: Skill; intelligence; the name of Lord Rama's mother in the Indian mythological epic Ramayana

Kaveri: Full of water; name of a sacred river in South India

Kavika: Female poet, from the word 'kavi' meaning 'poet'

*Kavita: Poem

Keemaya/Kimaya: Miracle; wonder; divine

Keerthi: Eternal fame; glory; reputation

Ketki/Ketaki: Name of a cream coloured, fragrant monsoon flower

Keya: Name of a flower

Khushbu: Fragrance; aroma

*Khushi: Happiness; cheer; delight

*Kiran: Ray/beam of light

Kishori: Little girl; minor

*Komal: Soft; tender; delicate

*Krisha/*Krishna: The dark skinned; name of a river in southern India; another name for Draupadi who married the five Pandavas in Mahabharata (Indian myth); another name for Goddess Durga

Krittika: Name of a star, the third nakashatra (lunar); the Pleiades constellation

Kruti: Creation; art; the act of doing; the action which is actually perceived and performed

Kshama: Flame; forgiveness; mercy

Kumuda: Joy of life; white water lily; red lotus

Kunti: Pandava's mother; one who gave birth to the Sun God's son, Karna

Kusum: Delicate flower; blossom

Kuvira: Courageous woman; warrior

L

Laasya: Name of a dance; the graceful movements of Bharatnatyam, the Classical Dance from southern India, performed by Goddess Parvati

Lajita: Modest; shy; humble

Lakshita: Distinguished; renowned; famous

*Lakshmi: Goddess Lakshmi is the Goddess of wealth, and wife of Lord Vishnu. Also prosperity; wealth; fortune; success; Lakshmi not only refers to financial wealth, but also intellectual and spiritual wealth; beauty

Lalana: A beautiful woman; a girl

Lali: Blushing; beloved; darling

Lalima: Blush; redness; glow; beauty; Lalima was the wife of Vishnu

Lalita: Beautiful woman; pleasant; playful; there is a Raga named 'Lalita-Gauri'

Lata: Creeper; vine; magnificent woman; Lata Mangeshkar is a living legend of Indian music – her name was entered in the Guinness Book of World Records (1984) as the singer with the largest number of songs to her name

Latika: Small creeper; red coloured dot on the forehead (kunku/bindi) of a woman to indicate that she is married (saubhagya-wati)

Leela/Lila: A dance drama; divine drama; game; cosmic play

*Leena/Lina: Devoted one; united; absorbed

Lipika: Letters; alphabets; manuscript; a short letter; 'Lipika' was a prose work written in Bengali by Rabindranath Tagore, the Nobel Laureate

M

Madhavi: Sweetness; as sweet as honey; derived from the word 'madhu' meaning 'honey'

Madhu: Honey; nectar; sweet; the wine of 'soma' (a divine drink)

Madhubala: Sweet woman; honey bee

Madhura: Sweet; pleasant; sugar

Madhuri: Sweetness; charming girl; Madhuri Dixit-Nene, a famous Bollywood actress, has won many awards for her acting talent

Magadhi: Another name for the Jasmin flower; a dialect; from 'Magadh' which was the capital of the prosperous empire during the seventh and eighth centuries BC

Mahika: The earth; dew drops

*Mahima: Divine glory; God's greatness; supremacy; one of the 'Astasiddhis'

Mahiya: Joy; happiness; ecstasy; love; derived from the word 'mahi' meaning 'the lover', because the legendary lover Ranjha was also known as Mahi

Maitreyi: Friendly, derived from the word 'maitri' meaning 'friendship'; 'Maitreyi' was the name of a wise and learned woman in ancient India

Maitri: Friendship; universal love and compassion; loving kindness

*Mala: String; garland; necklace

*Malaika: One from heaven; angel

*Malika: A flower; delicate garland

Malini: Fragrant; a female florist; name of a river

Malti/Malati: Moonlight; fragrant flower; blossom

Malvika/Malavika: One who lived in Malva. Malva is famous in Jain literature, as King Siddharaj's greatest victory was over Malva, a town in central India with unmatched literary tradition

Mamata: Motherly love; affection

Manali: A bird; one of the most beautiful adventure destinations in India, Manali is a small town in the Kullu valley of Himachal Pradesh. The Hindu lawgiver, Manu, first stepped on land here after the great deluge. It is said that the name Manali came from the term 'Manu-Alaya' meaning 'the home of Manu'

Manavi: Primal woman; wife of Manu; according to the Jain tradition, Goddess Manavi is the attendant Devi of the 10th Tirthankar, Sitalanath, who is known for his association with spiritual beings

Mandakini: Slow moving, derived from the word 'manda' meaning 'slow'; a river in ancient India

Mandavi: Capable manager; Mandavi was the wife of Bharat in the Indian myth Ramayana

Mandira: Dwelling place; pure; sacred like a temple; melody; cymbals (a musical instrument)

Manika: Jewel; bead; according to astrology this precious red stone (whose ruling planet is the sun) should be worn on the ring finger of the right hand to achieve fame, vigour, virtue, warmth and the capacity to command

Manini: Self-respect; self-esteem; derived from the word 'maan' meaning 'respect'

*#Manisha: Desire; wish; intellect; brilliance; Goddess of the mind

#Manju: Pleasant; beautiful; sweet

Manjusha: Jewellery box; treasure chest; derived from the Sanskrit word 'mani' meaning 'jewel'

Manjushri: Lady with a sweet voice; sweet lustre; beautiful; Manjushri is one of eight Bodhisattvas who took on the responsibility of explaining the limitless teachings of Buddha, and demonstrating their complete and accurate meanings; another name for Goddess Lakshmi

*Mansi/Manasi: Woman; born of the mind; Goddess of learning; another name for Goddess Saraswati; derived from the word 'manasa' meaning 'mind'

*#Maya: Illusion; magic; power of self-illusion; according to Indian mythology, the world is an illusion and 'Maya' is the power which creates this illusion

Mayuri: Pea hen; stringed musical instrument

Medha: Wisdom; intellect; brainpower; another name for Goddess Saraswati

#Meena/*Mina/#Minal: Precious gem; fish; the zodiac sign of Pisces is known as 'Meena' in Hindi

Meenakshi/Minakshi: One with beautiful fish-shaped eyes; another name for Goddess Parvati; the Meenakshi Sundareswarar temple in Madurai is one of the greatest Shiva temples in South India, known for its sprawling landscape filled with sculptural wonders

*Megha/Meghan/Meghana: Rain cloud; Raga Megha presents an image of blue-skinned Krishna blowing a conch to summon rain clouds, and is meant to be sung during the monsoon season

Mekhala: Slope of a mountain; belt; waistband

*Mili: A meeting; union; to find

*Mira/Meera: Ocean; sea; the name of Lord Krishna's devotee

#Meeta/Mita: Friend; measured

Mitali: Friendly one; friendship; derived from the word 'mita' meaning 'friend'

Mohini: Fascinating female; very beautiful, attractive, gorgeous; name of an apsara; name of the female form taken by Lord Vishnu

*Mona: Just one; alone

Monal: Bird

*Monika: Solitary; single; from the word 'mona' meaning 'alone'

*Monisha: Scholar; intelligent woman; solitary

Mridini: Good quality soil, derived from the word 'mrida' meaning 'clay'; another name for Goddess Parvati

Mridula: Tender; delicate; from the word 'mridu' meaning 'soft'

Mrinal/Mrinali: Lotus stem; tender

Mugdha: Innocent young girl; spellbound; bewildered

Mukta: One who is liberated, freed; rare pearl; derived from the word 'mukt' meaning 'to free' or 'to release', 'Mukta' is the state of a soul free from binding impurities, sins and sufferings

Mythri: Friendship; friend

N

*Naina: Eye

*Naiya: Water; boat; water nymph; 'Naiya-yikas' were the Indian logicians who validated the knowledge obtained and stated by their ancestors

Nalini: Lotus; sweet nectar; lovely

Namita: Humble; modest; derived from the word 'namana' meaning 'to bow'

Namrata: Politeness; bowing; gentleness; modesty

Nandana: Heavenly; cheerful; daughter; another name for Goddess Durga; according to Indian mythology, Nandana-vana (the heavenly gardens of Indra) was a forest famous for its beauty, said to be located between Mount Meru and Devakuru

*Nandini: Fabulous daughter; a divine cow that was able to fulfil all of the desires of those who worshipped her; another name for Goddess Durga

Nandita: Cheerful; pleasing

Narmada: A river; one who arouses tender feelings in others

*Natasha: Original one

Navika: New; young; captain/sailor-chief of a vessel

Navya: New; recent; fresh; novel; adorable; navya-nyaya is an ancient theory of word and sentence meaning

Nayana: Of the eye; pupil of the eye; one with attractive eyes

*Neelam: Blue sapphire. It is said that if one wears a flawless blue sapphire, it can remove poverty and provide health, wealth, long life, happiness and prosperity. An imperfect 'Neelam' is the cause of many miseries

Neepa: A flower

Neeraja: Lotus; pure; one with the qualities of water; another name for Goddess Lakshmi

#Neeta/#Neetu: Within rules; well-guided

*Neha: Loving; affectionate; friendly; rain

Neharika: Collection of stars; galaxy; Milky Way; dewdrops

Netra: Eye; one who exposes the truth; guide

*Nidhi: Wealth; treasure; prosperity

*Nikita: Victorious; successful

Nilima: Blue complexioned, derived from the word 'neel' meaning 'blue'

Nimisha: Momentary

Nimita: Fixed; determined

*Nina/Neena: Beautiful eyes; bejewelled; decorated

Nirali: Different; exclusive; one with unusual skills

Nirmala: Clean; pure; without any dirt; spotless; unsoiled

#Nirupama: Unique; matchless; incomparable

*#Nisha: Night; twilight

Nishita: Alert; quick; vigilant

Nitya: Eternal; immortal; another name for Goddess Durga

Nivedita: One devoted to the service of God

Niyati: Destiny; fortune; fate; another name for Goddess Durga

Nutan: New; fresh; young; modern

O

Oditi: Dawn; fresh

Ojal: Vision; revelation

Ojasvi: Bright; lustrous; one with radiant personality

Omisha: The Goddess of birth and death

Orpita: Offering

P

Padma: Lotus; another name for Goddess Lakshmi

Padmaja: One who is born from the lotus; another name for Goddess Lakshmi

Pahal: The start; beginning; commencement of life

Pallavi: Bud; tender; developing

Panita: Admired

Pankaja: Lotus; born in the mud

Pari/Parina: Fairy; as pretty as a fairy

Paridhi: Limit; boundary; periphery

Parinita: Expert; specialist; a married woman

Parmita: Wisdom; intelligence; knowledge

Parul: Graceful; elegant; beautiful

Parvati: Born of the mountain – derived from the word 'parvat' meaning 'mountain'; Parvati was the wife of Lord Shiva, known for her many forms

Parvini: Festival; celebration

Payal: Anklets; foot ornaments

Poonam: Full moon

Prabha: Light; radiance; splendour; shine

Prachi: East; morning

Pradnya: Wisdom; intelligence; knowledge

Prafula: In bloom; blooming

Pragati: Progress; development; growth

Prajakta: White coloured fragrant flower; mother of all mankind

Prama: Knowledge of truth; wisdom

Pramila: Less active; lethargic; the name of one of Arjuna's wives

Pranali: Organisation; system; policy; channel for movement of water (Sanskrit meaning)

Pranita: Promoted; advanced; led forward

Pratibha: Talent; intelligence; brightness; light

Pratika: Symbol; picture

Pratima: Idol; replica; statue

Praveena: Skilled; trained; capable

Prerna: Inspiration; encouragement

Priti/Preeti: Love; pleasure; affection; satisfaction

*****Priya**: Beloved; dear one

*****Priyanka**: One with whom you can easily fall in love

*****Puja/Pooja**: Prayer; ceremonial worship

Purnima: Full moon; the day of the full moon; glorious day

Purva: East; in front; elder

Pushpa: Flower; blossom

R

Rachana: Creation; arrangement

Radha: Prosperity; success; full moon day in the Hindu month of Vaishakh; personification of the absolute love for Lord Krishna

*Radhika: Successful; prosperous; another name for Radha

Rajashri: Royalty; sovereigns

Rajni: Night; dark; another name for Goddess Durga

Rajul: Brilliant; radiant; intelligent

Rakhi: Bond of protection; the thread tied by a sister to her brother during the festival of 'Rakhsha Bandhan' to ward off misfortune

Raksha: Protection; security; 'Raksha Bandhan' is a Hindu festival which honours the relationship between brothers and sisters, celebrated on the day of the full moon during the Hindu month of Shraavan

Ramita: Pleased; delighted

Ramya: Delightful; beautiful; enchanting; elegant

*Rani: Queen; Princess

Ranjana: Delighted; pleased

Ranjita: Amusing; entertaining

Rashi: A collection of wealth; zodiac sign

Rashmi: Rays of light; sunlight; moonlight

Rati: Joy; passion; love; wife of Kamdev, Lord of love

*Raveena: Sunny; fair skinned; derived from the word 'ravi' meaning 'sun'

*#Reema: White antelope; another name for Goddess Durga

*#Reena: Gem; pearl; precious stone

Rekha: Line; limit

Renuka: Atom; grain of sand; dust; mother of the sage Parshurama and wife of the sage Jamadagni

*Reshma: Silky; soft; smooth

Revathi: Wealthy; rich; brilliant; beautiful; the last of the 27 Nakshatras; the name of a star

*Rhea/Rhia: Flow of water; rivulet; stream

Richa: Hymn; the writing of Vedas, the Sanskrit verses; 'richa' is knowledge acquired through listening, and then repeating

Riddhi: Fortunate; wealthy; prosperous; the wife of Lord Ganesha

*Rita/#Reeta: Standard of living; lifestyle

#Ritu: Season

Riya: Singer

*Rohini: Name of a divine cow; the fourth of the 27 Nakshatras meaning 'a red cow'; the name of a star

Roma: One with shiny hair; another name for Goddess Lakshmi

*Roshni: Light; brightness

Rucha/Ruchita: Brightness; brilliance; radiance; Vedic lyrics

Ruchi: Taste; liking; pleasure

Ruchika/Ruchira: Lustrous; tasteful; pleasing

Ruhi: Soul; spirit; rising

*Rupa/Roopa: Beauty; form; silver

Rupal: Made of silver

Rupali/Roopali: Beautiful girl; pretty; derived from the word 'roopa' meaning 'beautiful'

Rupika: Silver coin; one with good looks

Rutva: Speech; verbal communication

S

Sachi: Grace; help; the name of the wife of Lord Indra

*#Sadhana: Long worship; the practice of spiritual self-training and exercise through which perfection is attained

Sadhika: One who accomplishes her goal with the help of 'Sadhana' (see above); another name for Goddess Durga

Sagarika: Wave; one born in the ocean – derived from the word 'sagar' meaning 'ocean'

Saheli: Friend; companion

Sajani: Beloved; favourite; dear

Sakshi: Witness; evidence

Saloni: Beautiful; good-looking

*Sameera: The fresh smell of the early morning; name of a flower; pleasant

Sampada: Wealthy; prosperous; another name for Goddess Lakshmi

Sanchali: Movement; mobility

*Sandhya: Twilight; evening; early morning

*Sanjana: In harmony; realization; well-informed; wise

Sanyukta: Relating to; united; joined

*Sara: Precious; valuable

Sarla: Straightforward; honest; simple

Sarika: A singing bird; a Myna bird; natural beauty

Sarita: River; flowing; another name for Goddess Durga

Saroj/Saroja: Lotus flower

Sarojini: Pond full of lotuses; abundance of lotuses; Sarojini Naidu was one of the most famous freedom fighters of India

Saruchi: Wonderful; marvellous; fabulous

Sarupa: Beautiful; good looking; with form; derived from the base word 'rupa' meaning 'beauty', adding 'sa' at the front means 'with' or 'to have'

Saumyaa: Gentle; calm; a flower; another name for Goddess Durga

*Savera: Dawn; morning; beginning; ray of hope

Savita: The sun

Savitri: A river; power of the sun; another name for Goddess Saraswati; Savitri fought with Yama, the God of death, and brought her husband back to life

Sayali: The name of a flower

*#Seema: Border; limit; ethics

*Sejal: River water; pure

*Shaila: One who lives in the mountains; Goddess

Shailaja: Daughter of the mountain; river; another name for Goddess Parvati

Shalaka: Pointed stick; sharp; another name for Goddess Parvati

*Shalini: Modest; humble; house-wife

*Shama/Shamila: Equal; evenly distributed; calm

Shambhavi: Sacred grass with blue flowers; Goddess Durga

*Shanti: Peace; calm

*Sharda/Sharada: The Goddess of learning; one who holds the Vina (musical instrument), Goddess Saraswati; another name for Goddess Durga

Sharini: Earth

#Sharmila: Shy; coy; modest

Sharvari: Twilight; dusk

Sheela/Sheila: Character; one with good morals; virtuous; calm

Sheetal: Cool; pleasant

Shefali: Fragrant; a flower

Shikha: Top; peak; tip; flame

Shilpa: Perfectly created; well-balanced; sculpture

Shivangi: Beautiful; gorgeous

*#Shivani: Another name for Goddess Parvati, the wife of Lord Shiva

Shobha: Beauty; grace; splendour

Shobhana: Shining; glowing; beautiful

*Shona: Redness; fiery; heat

Shraddha: Faith; trust; loyalty; devotion; total commitment

*Shreya: Auspicious; beautiful; best

Shristi: Nature; scenery; environment

*Shruti: Knowledge of Vedas; musical pitch; hearing

Shubhangi: Beautiful; attractive; derived from the combination of 'shubh' meaning 'good' and 'anga' meaning 'body'

Shweta: White; fair complexioned

Siddhi: Achievement; accomplishment of a goal; extraordinary power; the wife of Lord Ganesh

*Simran: God's gift

#Sita/#Seeta: White; stunning woman; the wife of Lord Rama

Smita: Always smiling; blossoming

Smruti: Memory; remembrance

*Sneha: Love; affection

Snehal: One who brings love to people; full of affection

Snigdha: Affectionate; friendly; soft; tender

*#Sonal/Sonali/Sonia: Someone who possesses the qualities of gold, derived from the word 'sona' meaning 'gold'

Subhadra: Glorious; magnificient; Subhadra was the wife of Arjuna in the Indian mythological epic Mahabharata; another name for Goddess Durga

Sucheta: One with a good mind; extremely clever; alert

Suchita: Auspicious; holy

Suchitra: Good painting; wonderful picture; derived from the base word 'chitra' meaning 'portrait' or 'beautiful', and 'su' at the beginning meaning 'good'

Sudha: Nectar; honey; 'Sudha' is the name of a spiritual drink which is said to make the drinker immortal. According to the Indian myth Mahabharata, Sudha was made in the ocean during Samudra Manthan (ocean churning)

*Suman: One with a pure heart; flower; charming

Sumati: Good mind; thoughts that lead to welfare; blessed with wisdom

Sumedha: Intelligent; wise; highly sensible

Sumitra: Good friend; very friendly; Sumitra was the mother of Lakshmana according to the Indian mythological epic Ramayana

Sunanda: Pleasing; good charactered; the name of a divine cow in the history of Lord Rama's ancestor, King Dilip

Sunayana: Beautiful eyed; derived from the words 'nayana' meaning 'of the eye' and 'su' meaning 'beautiful'

#Sunita: Well behaved; one with good ethics

Supriya: One who is loved by everyone; beloved

Surabhi: Fragrance; perfume; aroma; another name for the divine cow, Kamdhenu, who could grant wishes

Sushma: Exceptionally beautiful woman

#Sushmita: One with a charming smile

#Suvarna: Meaning gold or golden, 'suvarna' is a Sanskrit word for 'gold'

Swapna/Sapna: Dream; dream-like

Swati: The self-moving one; the 15th of the 27 Nakshatras; the name of a star

T

*Tamanna: Wish; desire; hope

*Tania/Tanaya/Tanuja/Taniya: Daughter; a perfect fit in one's family

*Tanisha: Ambition; aspiration

Tanmaya: Absorbed; devoted

Tanushree: Beautiful

*Tanvee/Tanvi: Slender; beautiful; delicate; young; another name for Goddess Durga

*Tara: Star

Tarana: Composition; song; invented by Amir Khusru, 'Tarana' is a type of music made up of a very quick succession of notes

Tarani: Boat; one who helps others in difficulties

*Tarika: One who belongs to the stars; divine

Tarulata: Creeper

Taruna: Young girl; fresh; blossom

Teekshna: Sharp witted; penetrative qualities

Tejasvi: Energetic; brilliant; lustrous; glowing

Tithi: Dates of the Hindu calendar

Toral: A folk heroine

Tripti: Satisfaction; fulfilment

*Trisha/Trishna: Thirst; wish; desire

Trishala: Trident, a three-pronged spear; making thirsty; desiring; the mother of Lord Mahavira, the 24th Tirthankara of Jainism

Triveni: The meeting point of the three sacred rivers, Ganga, Yamuna and Saraswati; fertile land; prosperous area

Triya: Young girl; adolescent girl

*Tulsi/Tulasi: The incomparable one; the name of a sacred basil plant, the 'Tulsi' plant is worshipped by the Hindu household to bring harmony, peace and happiness to the home

Turanya: Swift; quick; horse

Turvi: Superior

Tvisha: Bright; splendid

U

Udantika: Satisfaction; contentment

Udayati: Elevated; daughter of 'Udaya' – 'udaya' means 'to rise' or 'prosper', thus 'Udayati' means 'full of prosperity', or 'ascending to new heights'

Udita: One who has risen; one who has prospered

Uditi: Rising; one on the path to success

Ujvhala/Ujjwala: Light; brightness; lustrous

*Uma: Tranquility; brightness; light; lady of the mountain; another name for Goddess Parvati, wife of Lord Shiva

Unnati: Progress; development; evolution

Upasna: Worship; veneration; homage

Urmi: Wave; ripple; tide

#Urmila: Enchantress; beautiful; wife of Lakshmana (Lord Rama's brother in the Indian myth Ramayana)

Urvashi: Name of an Apsara; beauty; celestial; another name for the River Ganges

Urvi: The earth

Usha: Dawn; sunrise

Utkarsha: Advancement; prosperity; excellence

Uttara: Higher; superior; the name of a star; the 12th of the 27 Nakshatras, also known as 'Uttara Phalguni', meaning 'the excellent one'; the wife of Abhimanyu, Arjuna's son in the mythological epic Mahabharata

$\mathcal{V}$

Vahini: Flowing; conveyer; carrier

Vaidehi: Princess of Videha; another name for Sita, the wife of Lord Rama, from the Indian mythological epic Ramayana

Vaijayanti: Prize; banner; Lord Vishnu's garland

Vaishali: The noble one; name of a historic city

*Vaishnavi: Worshipper of Lord Vishnu; name of a Goddess

Vamaa/Vama: Beautiful; woman; the left side; another name for Goddess Durga; the mother of Parshvanatha, the 23rd Jain Tirthankara

Vamika: Left aligned; another name for Goddess Durga

Vanalika: Sunflower; belonging to the forest, derived from the word 'vana' meaning 'forest'

Vandana: To bow with respect; worship; salutation

Vanini: Softly spoken; wise woman; derived from the word 'vani' meaning 'speech'

Vanita: Lady; woman; loved one

Vanmayi: Expert in speaking skills. According to Sanskrit literature, one who is 'vani-maya' ('full of speech') is Vanmayi; another name for Goddess Saraswati

Vanshika: Flute; a musical instrument

*Varada: One who grants wishes; daughter; a river; another name for Goddess Lakshmi

Varali: Moon; the name of a Raga

Varalika: One who controls the army; the powerful one; another name for Durga, Goddess of power

Varidhi: Full of water; ocean; formed from the base word 'vari' meaning 'water'

Varija: Born in water; lotus

#Varsha: Rain; the monsoon season

Vartika: The offering of a lighted lamp to God

Varuni: Like water; derived from 'varun' meaning 'Lord of water'

Vasanti: Belonging to the spring season; light yellow colour; name of a Ragini

Vasuda/Vasudha: One who gives wealth; another name for earth

Vasundhara: One who has wealth; wealthy; another name for earth

Vatsala: One who has affection for children; loving

Vedanti: One who knows Vedas

Vedha: Pious; religious

Vedika: Consciousness; fence; railing

Veena/#Vina: Flute; a musical instrument

Venya: Lovable; adorable

Vibha: Light; radiant; glory

Vibhuti: Miraculous power; divine powers; another name for Goddess Lakshmi

Vidhi: The exact method of worship; Goddess of destiny

Vidisha: Name of a town in Madhya Pradesh, a state in India; the Jain heritage centre where the famous 'Sanchi Stupa' is situated

Vidula: Moon

Vidya: Knowledge; wisdom; another name for Goddess Saraswati

Vijayalakshmi: Victorious; the Goddess of victory

Vimala: Clean; pure

Vinaya: Humble; modest

Vinita: One who respects others; modest

Vishakha: Stars; multi branched one; 16th of the 27 Nakshatras

Vividha: Different; one with different qualities

#Vrinda: Another name for Tulsi, the sacred basil plant; another name for Goddess Radha

Vrishti: Rain; shower; abundance

Vritika: Thought; notion

W

Wakeeta: Beautiful flower

Y

Yachana: Plead; request

Yamini: Nocturnal; of the night

Yamuna: The name of a holy river

Yashasvi/Yashaswini: One who is successful; the Goddess of success

Yashoda: One who grants fame; the foster mother of Lord Krishna; the wife of Tithankara Mahavira (according to Jain beliefs)

Yashodhara: One who has achieved fame; the wife of Lord Buddha

Yavana: Quick; swift

Yogini: One with magical powers; fairy; one who can control senses

Yogita: A female disciple; enchanted

Yugandhara: Strongest; toughest

Yukta: Attentive; clever; engrossed with; with skills

Yuti: Union; coming together; merger

Yutika: Large in number; a flower; union of many; derived from the base word 'yuti' meaning 'union'

Yuvana: Young; physically fit; healthy

Hindu Twin Names

Boy – Boy

Akash – Prakash

Abhay – Ajay

Abhay – Akshay

Ajay – Vijay

Akhil – Nikhil

Amit – Sumit

Anil – Sunil

Anurag – Anup

Arun – Varun

Ashok – Nishok

Ayush – Piyush

Chetan – Ketan

Chirag – Anurag

Chirag – Chetan

Chirag – Parag

Dheeraj – Neeraj

Divit – Vinit

Gaurav – Saurav

Harish – Girish

Hemant – Sumant

Hiren – Dhiren

Luv – Kush

Mahesh – Naresh

Mayur – Mayank

Mukesh – Suresh

Narendra – Surendra

Rajesh – Rakesh

Ritesh – Yogesh

Rohit – Mohit

Sandeep – Pradeep

Varun – Tarun

Vinod – Pramod

Vinod – Vishal

Vipin – Nitin

Boy – Girl

Akshay – Akshita

Amit – Ambika

Aniruddha – Anuradha

Anuj – Anuja

Anuj – Anushka

Raju – Manju

Vijay – Vina

Girl – Girl

Amala – Kamala

Amisha – Manisha

Amrita – Ankita

Anita – Sunita

Anjali – Gitanjali

Anjana – Aparna

Anju – Manju

Anupama – Nirupama

Aparna – Suvarna

Archana – Aparna

Asha – Nisha

Asmita – Sushmita

Gita/Geeta – Sita/Seeta

Harsha – Varsha

Himani – Shivani

Maya – Chaaya

Meena – Reena

Meeta – Neeta

Neeta – Reeta

Nisha – Esha

Ritu – Neetu

Sadhana – Aradhana

Seema – Reema

Sonal – Minal

Urmila – Sharmila

Vrinda – Brinda

Muslim Names

The Prophet Muhammad recommended that Muslims should be selective when choosing the names of their children, as part of the identity of being a Muslim. He recommended that the most beautiful names are those which give servitude or praise to Allah.

Therefore, the child should be named after one of the ninety-nine names of Allah, or after the names of Prophets as mentioned in the Quran.

Names which suggest ill-omens or have bad meanings, or the names of wicked people, are frowned upon.

Muslim Boys' Names

A

Aariz: Brilliant; reputed

*Abbas: One with the characteristics of a lion

*Abdul: Servant of Allah

*Abdul-Aziz: Servant of the mighty, the powerful; derived by combining two words, 'abdul' meaning 'servant', and 'aziz' meaning 'mighty'; son of Abdullah al-Hashim, the amir of Makkah and leader of the Pilgrims

Abdul-Baari: Servant of the inventor

Abdul-Ghafoor: Servant of the forgiver; servant of the kind-hearted

Abdul-Haafiz: Servant of the protector; servant of the guardian

Abdul-Hameed: Servant of the praiseworthy or honourable one

Abdul-Haseeb: Servant of the respected one

Abdul-Jabaar: Servant of the dominant one

Abdul-Khaaliq: Servant of the creator

Abdul-Qaadir: Servant of the capable; servant of the able or skilled

*Abdul-Raheem: Servant of the most empathetic, kind-hearted

*Abdul-Rahman: Servant of the most merciful

Abdul-Rasheed: Servant of the one who guides the way

Abdul-Razaaq: Servant of the maintainer, one who provides the necessities of life

Abdul-Salaam: Servant of harmony

Abdul–Waahid: Servant of the One; slave of the unique; son of Zayd and a disciple of Hasan al-Basri, Abdul-Waahid was a preacher and ascetic who died at Basrah

*Abdullah/Abdallah/Abdulla: Servant of Allah; the father of the Prophet Mohammed

Abed: One who worships Allah

*Abrahim: Father of a multitude; earth; a Prophet's name

*Abu: Father

*Adil/Adeel/Aadil: Justice; honesty; fairness

*Adnan: Tribal ancestor of the Prophet

Agha: Chief; master; lord; another name for Allah

Aheed: One who takes something aside; one of the Prophet's names

*Ahmed/Ahmad: Praiseworthy; worth appreciating; one who is admirable; one of the names of the Prophet

*Ahsan: Act of kindness; favour; kind help

*Akil/Aqeel: Wise; intelligent; Abu Aqeel was a transcriber of the Quran

*Akim: One who believes in Allah

*Akram: Most generous; very kind; another name for Allah; Wasim Akram, a Pakistani cricket player, is one of the fastest and most successful bowlers in the world

*Ali: Excellent; noble; dignified; one of the ninety-nine names of Allah

Alif: The first character in the Arabic alphabet Hijaiyah. Each letter has a numerical value. This is called the 'Neptu Huruf Hijaiyah'

*Alim/Aleem: Wise; scholar; knowledgeable; one of the names of Allah

*Amaan/Aman: Protection; guard; security

*Ameen/Amin: Faithful; trustworthy; honest; one of the names of the Prophet

*#Amir/Aamir: Rich; prosperous; wealthy; Aamir Khan is a famous Bollywood actor whose film, 'Lagaan', was nominated for an Oscar in 2002

Amjad: Glorious; celebrated; famous

*#Anees/Anis: Dear friend; companion

*Anwar: Radiant; the brightest; light

*Aqib/Aqeeb: Descendant; follower; last in the succession of the Prophets

*Areeb: Skilful; expert; intelligent

*Arif/Aarif: Well–informed; knowledgeable

*#Armaan: Wish; desire

Ashfaq: Gracious prince; noble prince

*#Ashraf: More respectable; most noble; superior

*Asif: Forgiveness; pardon; mercy

*#Asim/Aasim: Guardian; defender; protector; name of one of the famous reciters of the Quran. Also an Ansar companion, son of Thabit, an early Islamic Poet

*Atif: Compassionate; sympathetic

Atiq: Independent; Ibn Abu Atiq was a patron of singing

*Ayaz: The slave of Mehmood Gaznawi

*Ayoob/Ayub: One who asks for pardon; one who apologises; a Prophet's name

*Azan: Azan is the first call to prayer, uttered in a loud voice by the Muezzin to announce the time for the Obligatory Prayer and to invite everybody to offer the same

*Azeem/#Azim: Grand; big; mighty; one of the ninety-nine names of Allah

Azeez: One who is dear; a friend; comrade; a Prophet's name

*Azhar: The shiniest; brightest

Azzam: Determined; resolved; firm

B

Baahir: Brilliant; highly radiant

Baasim: Smiling; happy; joyful; cheerful

Baasit: One who spreads prosperity; one of the ninety-nine names of Allah

Badrudeen/Badr Udeen: The full moon of the faith; derived by combining two words, 'badr' meaning 'full moon' and 'udeen' meaning 'faith'

Bashaar: One who brings happy news; giver of good news; Prophet's name

Basheer/Bushraa: Good news; happy news; good omen

Basir: Wise; prudent; intelligent; one of the ninety-nine names of Allah

*Bilal: The Prophet's companion who calls people to prayer; the name of the first Muezzin

D

Daai: One who calls for prayers; one of the names of the prophet Muhammad

*Dawood/Dawoud/Daud/Daoud: Another name for the Prophet David

Diyaa–Udeen: The lamp of faith; derived by combining 'diya' meaning 'lamp' and 'udeen' meaning 'faith'

E

Eemaan: Strong belief; unshakeable faith in Allah and the religion

*Ehsaan: Favour; help; kindness

*Eshan: Desire; wish; aim

F

Faakhir: Proud; derived from the word 'fakr' meaning 'pride'

*Faisal/Faysal: Decision maker; arbitrator

*Faiyaz: Artistic; inventive

*Faiz/Faizan/Faysan: Gain; profit maker

*Faraz: Altitude; ascent

*Fardeen: The light of religion

Fareed/Farid: Unique; pearl; alone

Farhad: The one who digs mines or cuts stone

*Farhan: Glad; merry; joyful

Farooq/Faruq: One who distinguishes truth from falsehood

*Farukh: Power of discrimination or separation; auspicious

Fateen/Faatin: Charming; fascinating; intelligent; smart

Fateh: Victory; the name of a Prophet

Fatik: Crystal

Fazal: Grace; able; intelligent; wise

Firoz/Firoze/Fairoze: Precious stone; winner; successful

G

Ghaalib: Victor; champion; dominant

Ghaazi: Conqueror; hero; captor

Ghauth/Ghiyaath: One who listens to complaints; helper; succour; the name of a Prophet

Ghufran: Forgiving; pardon; another name for Allah

Gulab: The rose

*Gulam/Ghulam: Servant; slave of Allah

Gulshan: Garden of flowers

ℋ

*Haamid: One who praises Allah; one of the ninety-nine names of Allah; one of the names of the Prophet

*Haashim: Kindness; humanity; Prophet's grandfather

Haashir: The gatherer; one of the names of the Prophet

Haatim: Judge; determined one; unavoidable

*Habib: Beloved; dearly loved; one of the names of the Prophet

Hafiz: Protector; one who guards; one who knows the Quran by heart; one of the ninety-nine names of Allah; one of the Prophet's names

*Haider/Hayder: Lion; king of the jungle

*Hakeem/Hakim: Healer; physician; a Muslim sage; wise; intelligent; one of the ninety-nine names of Allah; another name for the Quran

*Hammad/Hamad/Hamaad: One who praises God (loudly)

Hamshad: Always victorious

*Hamza/Hamazah: Lion

*Haneef/Hanif: True believer; orthodox

*Haroon/Harun: Exalted; superior; hope; derived from the original word 'aaron'; Harun al-Rashid was a 9th-century Abbasid caliph featured in the stories of 'The 1001 Nights'; a prophet's name

Hashmat: Glory; dignity

*Hasib: Respected and esteemed one; one of the ninety-nine names of Allah; another name for the Prophet

*Hassan/Hasan: Handsome; beautiful; good; the grandson of the Prophet Muhammad

Hayaam: Deeply in love

Houd/Hud: Right guidance; a Prophet's name

Humam: Kind and courageous

Husaam/Husam: Sword

*Hussein/Hussain/Huseyin: Handsome; Islamic thinker; saint; the grandson of the Prophet Muhammad, Hasan was Husein's older brother

I

*Ibrahim/Ibraaheem/Ebrahim: Father of many; earth; Prophet's name (Abraham)

*Idrees: A Prophet's name

Iesa: A Prophet's name

*Ihsaan/Ihsan: Benevolence; kindness; charity

*Ikram: Honour; respect

*Ilyas: Derived from the Hebrew name 'Eliyahu' meaning 'my God is Yahweha'; a Prophet's name

*Imaad/Imad: Support; assurance; pillar

Imaad Udeen: The pillar of faith

*Imam: Leader; chief

*Iman/Imaan: Faith; belief; derived from Arabic word 'amana' meaning 'to believe'

*Imraan (Imran): Strong; long-lived; Imran Khan is a famous Pakistani all-round cricketer and legendary fast bowler. He captained Pakistan in the cricket World Cup in 1992, which they won; a Prophet's name

Imtiaz/Imtiyaz: Power of discrimination; privilege

Inas: Sociability; care

Inayat: Kindness; favour; reward

Intekhab/Intikhab: Chosen; selected

Iqbal: Prosperous; fortunate

*#Irfaan: Thankfulness; gratefulness; knowledge

Irshaad: Guidance; supervision; direction

*Isaam: Safeguard; security; protection

*Ishaan: The sun; fire

*Is-haaq: A prophet's name

Ishrat: Affection; happiness; companionship

*Ismaael/Ismail: One who is heard by Allah; a Prophet's name

Izhar: Submission; exposure; declaration

J

Jaabir: Consoler; comforter; a Prophet's name

Jaafar: Rivulet; stream

Jabbaar: Dominant; powerful; strong; one of the ninety-nine names of Allah

Jabez: Sorrow; grief

Jalaal: Famous; important; glory

Jalil: Grand; majestic; one of the ninety-nine names of Allah

*Jameel: Good mannered; courteous; polite

Jashan: Celebration

*#Javed: Immortal; long-lived

Jawad: Free handed; generous; plentiful; ample

Jihan: The world; universe

*Junaid/Juned: Soldier; warrior; fighter

K

*Kabir: Grand; great; one of the ninety-nine names of Allah; the name of a sage who wrote many Hindi hymns

Kadeem: Slave to God; servant

Kadir: Green like grass; the green colour of Spring, depicting freshness and innocence

Kahil: Best friend; lover

#Kaif: Joy; pleasure

*Kaleem/Kaleemullah: One who converses with Allah; speaker; Prophet's name

Kamal: Perfection; precision

*Kareem/#Karim/Kerim: Kind;   generous;   merciful;   noble; respected; 'Ramadan karim' is a phrase meaning 'blessed Ramadan' (Ramadan is the Muslim month of fasting); one of the ninety-nine names of Allah; one of the Prophet's names

*Kashif: Discoverer; one who reveals

*Kasim/Kazim: One who can control anger

*Kazi/Qazi: One who can control anger; one who conducts prayers in a mosque

Khadim: Servant of Allah

*Khaleel/Khalil: Trustworthy friend; honest companion; name of a Prophet

*Khalid/Khaled: Eternal; immortal

*Khan: Prince; leader

*Khatib: Preacher; speaker

L

Labeeb: Sensible; rational; wise

Latif/Lateefa: Gentle; kind; friendly; one of the ninety-nine names of Allah

Luqmaan: A prophet's name

M

Maahir: Skilled

*Mahmoud/Mahmud: One who is praised; one of the names of the Prophet

Mahtab: Moon; pleasant; calm

*Majeed/#Majid: Glorious; famous; of high status; one of the ninety-nine names of Allah; one of the names of the Quran, the holy book of the Muslims

Makaarim: Well-mannered; one with an honourable character

Makeen: Strong; firm; a Prophet's name

*Malik: The king; the monarch; one of the ninety-nine names of Allah

Mamdouh: One who is admired; praised; glorified

Mamoon: Trustworthy; responsible; a Prophet's name

*Mansoor/Mansour: Aided by God; victorious; a Prophet's name

Marzouq: Blessed by God; privileged

*Masoud: Happy; lucky; fortunate

Maysarah: Effortless; comfort

Mehboob: Beloved; dear

*Mirza: A prince; monarch

Misbaah: Shining; lamp; light; a Prophet's name

Moazzem: The respected one; honourable

*Momin: One who believes in God; one of the ninety-nine names of Allah

Moosa: A Prophet's name

Muayid: Supported; maintained

*Mubarak: Congratulations; holy; sacred

Mufeed: Helpful; co-operative

*Muhammad/Mohammad/Muhmmad/Mohammed/Muhmed:
Praiseworthy; one who is praised; derived from the Arabic word 'hamida' which means 'to praise'; the name of the last Prophet, Muhammad was a direct descendant of Ismail, the first son of Prophet Ibrahim (Abraham); Muhammed was the name of the prophet who founded the Islamic religion in the 7th century; this name (with all of its variants) is probably the most popular in the world

*Muhsin: Beneficient; generous

*Mujaahid: Fighter; warrior; soldier

Mujeeb: One who accepts answers; respondent; a Prophet's name

*Mukhtaar: Chosen one; a Prophet's name

*Muneer/Munir: Brilliant; shining; bright; one of the Prophet's names

Muqtaf: Successor; the selected one; a Prophet's name

Musaddaq: Confirmer; truthful; one of the names of the Prophet

Musharraf/#Musharaf: Honoured; respected; dignified; General Pervez Musharraf appointed himself as Pakistan's president on 20th June 2001

Musheer: Adviser; counsellor

*Mustafa/Mustapha: The chosen one; a Prophet's name; Mustafa Kamal was the founder of modern Turkey

Muwafaq: Victorious; triumphant

Naail: Acquirer; earner; attainer

Naasih: Mentor; adviser; a Prophet's name

Naathim: Co-ordinator; adjuster

Nabeeh/Nabhan/Nabeel: Noble; exceptional; glorious; one of the Prophet's names

*Nadeem/Nadim: Friend; drinking companion; from the Arabic word 'nadama' which means 'to drink'

*Nadir/Naadir: Rare; precious

Nadwa: Council; committee; board

*Naeem/Naim: Comfort; effortless; relaxing

*Nahid: Eminent; superior

Najaah: Success; victory; triumph

Najat: Safety; security; protection

*Najeeb/Najib: Of noble descent; intelligent; wise

Najm Udeen: The star of the faith

*Naseem/#Nasim: Fresh air; breeze

*Nasir/Naseer: One who helps; one who protects; a Prophet's name

Nasir Udeen: The protector of the faith

Natheer: One who gives warnings

#Naved: Good news

Nawfal: Charitable; kind

Nazeeh: Pure; virtuous

Nazeem/#Nazim: Co-ordinator; organiser

Nooh: Wisdom; intelligence; a Prophet's name

*Noor: Light; from the Arabic word 'nawara' which means 'to illuminate'; one of the names of the Prophet

Noor Udeen: Brightness of the faith

O

*Omar/*Omair/Omer: Life; long-lived

Omran: Firm construction

*Osama: Courageous and brave like a lion

*Osman/Usman: Name of a bird; name of the third caliph of the Muslims; Muhammad's son-in-law

P

Parvez: Victorious

Pirmohammed: Holy Prophet

Q

*Qasim: One who is just and equitable; one who shares with others; derived from the Arabic word 'qasama' which means 'to share' or 'to divide'; a Prophet's name; name of Prophet Mohammed's son

Qayyim: Equitable; strong; one of the names of the Prophet; another name for the Quran

Quamar: The moon

Quasar: Meteor

Qudamah: Bravery

Quddus: One who is pure; the holy one; one of the ninety-nine names of Allah

Qutub: Tall; pole; celebrity

ℛ

Raakin: Respectful; courteous

Raamiz: Symbol; sign

Raatib: One who arranges; organiser

Rabab: Clouds

Rafeeq: Kind; gentle; friend; companion

*Rafi: Exalted; dignified; glorious; one of the ninety-nine names of Allah

Ragheb: Desirous; keen

*Raheel/Rahil: One who shows the way; traveller

*Raheem/#Rahim: Merciful; kind-hearted; one of the ninety-nine names of Allah

Rajab: The seventh month of the Muslim year

Rashad: Good guidance; good sense

*Rashid: Rightly guided; mature; one of the ninety-nine names of Allah; a Prophet's name

Rasul/Rasool: Messenger; preacher; derived from the verb 'arsala' meaning 'to send', hence Rasul is 'the one who was sent'; a Prophet's name

*Raza: Pleasure; will; derived from Arabic word 'riza' meaning 'satisfaction'

Razzaq: One who sustains; one who provides the necessities of life; one of the ninety-nine names of Allah

*#Rehman/Rahman: The most merciful; kind; one of the ninety-nine names of Allah

*Ridhwan/*Rizvan: Goodwill; reputation; one who brings good news

*Riyadh: Gardens

Riyaz: Practice; training

Rushan/Roshan: Illuminated; bright; light

S

*Saabir: Patient; calm; tolerant

*#Saajid: One who worships God; one who lies on the ground as a sign of respect

Saalih: Virtuous; righteous; honourable

*Sadeeq/Sadiq: Honest; truthful; name of a Prophet

*Saeed/Syed/Seyed: Happy; heavenly; holy

*Sahib: Companion; friend; follower

*Sahil: River bank; shore; coast

*#Saif: Sword

Saifullah: The sword of Allah

Salah/Saliah: Righteous; virtuous; a Prophet's name

*Saleem/Salim/Selim/#Salman: Safe; derived from the Arabic word 'salima', meaning 'to be safe'

Salil: Descendant; son

*Sameen/Samin: Valuable; precious

Sameer/Samir: Entertaining companion; companion in the evening

*Saquib/Sakib: Bright; intelligent

Sarfaraz: Respected; admired

*Sayid/Sayed: Master; leader; chief; one of the names of the Prophet

*Shaahid: Sacrificial victim; martyr; patriot; one of the ninety-nine names of Allah; Prophet's name

*Shafeeq/Shafiq: Compassionate; soft; tender; the name of a Prophet

*Shahbaz: King of Falcons

Shaheer: Famous; renowned; one of the Prophet's names

*Shakeel: Handsome; good-looking

Shakib: Tolerance; patience

*Shakir: Grateful; thankful

Shamim: Aroma; fragrance

Shareef: Distinguished; noble; name of a Prophet

Shariq: Intelligent; radiant

*Sheikh/Shaikh: Leader; chief; teacher

*Shoaib/Shuaib/Shohaib: A Prophet's name

*Siraaj: Lamp; light; name of a Prophet

*Sohail/Suhail: Name of a star; moon glow; derived from 'Suhail', the Arabic name for the second brightest star in the sky, Canopus

*Suhayb: One with red hair or complexion

*Sulayman/Suleman/Sulaimaan: Peace; a Prophet's name

*Sultan: King; ruler

$\mathcal{T}$

*Taahir: Clean; pure; a Prophet's name

Taj: Crown; jewel

Talal: Admirable; marvellous; good

Talat: Prayer; a form of worship

Talib: Seeker of knowledge; student

Tamam: Charitable; kind

Tanseem: Divine gesture

*Tanveer/Tanwir: Enlightening; revealing; illuminating

Tareef: Rare; unusual; unique

*Tariq/Tarik/Tareq: He who pounds at the door; name of a morning star; Tariq was the name of the Islamic military leader who occupied Spain; a Prophet's name

Tawfeeq: Good fortune; success; derived from the Arabic word 'wafiqa' meaning 'to be successful'

*Tayyab/Taayib/Tayyeb: Good; nice; one of the Prophet's names

Thaqib: Penetrating; sharp; shooting star

U

Ubaidah: Servant of God

*Umar: Blooming; thriving; derived from Arabic word 'amara' meaning 'to thrive'; name of the second Caliph

Usama/Usaamah: Lion; king of the jungle

*Usman: A baby bird; name of the third Caliph

W

*#Waahid/Waheed: Matchless; unique; single; exclusive; unequalled; one of the ninety-nine names of Allah; one of the names of the Prophet

Wafeeq: Flourishing; successful

Wahab: Giver; generous; donor

Wajeeh: Noble; eminent; a Prophet's name

Waleed: Newborn child; derived from Arabic word 'walada' meaning 'to give birth'

Waliyuddeen: Follower of the faith

*Waqar: Dignity; sobriety

*Waris: Heir; inheritor

*Waseem/Wasim: Graceful; good-looking

$\mathcal{Y}$

*Yaaseen: Chief; leader; one of the Prophet's names; one of the Surahs in the Quran

Yafiah: High; elevated

Yahyaa: Gracious; a Prophet's name

Yasaar: Ease; rich; lavish

*Yasir/Yaseer: Wealthy; prosperous

Yazeed: To grow; to enhance; to develop

*Yunus/Yonis/Yunis/Younis: A bird; a Prophet's name; derived from the Hebrew word 'yonah' meaning 'dove'

*Yusuf/Yousif: A Prophet's name; derived from the Hebrew name 'Yoseph' which means 'he will add'

$\mathcal{Z}$

*Zaafir: Triumphant; victorious

*#Zaahid: Self-disciplined; ascetic

*#Zaahir: Bright; shining

Zaigham: Lion; king of the jungle

*Zakariya/Zakariah: Derived from the Hebrew name 'Zekaryah' which means 'the Allah remembers'; a Prophet's name

*Zakir: One who remembers God repeatedly

Ziyad: Abundance; development

*Zuhair/Zuhayr: Bright; intelligent; clever; 'Zuhair' was the name of a 6th century Arab poet, considered the greatest poet of pre-Islamic times

Muslim Girls' Names

A

*Aafreen: Brave; courageous

*Aalia/*Aaliya: Glorious; highest social standing; dignified

*Aasmaa: Valuable; precious

Ablaa: Perfectly created; one with a good figure

*Adeela: Equal; just; derived from the Arabic word 'adala' meaning 'to act justly'

*Afsana: Fiction; fairy tale

*Aisha/*Ayesha/Aishah/Ayisha: Prosperous; flourishing; the wife of Prophet Mohammed

*Alia/Aaliyah: Exalted; high

*Alisha/Alyssa/Alysha/Alesha/Aleisha/Alisa/Aliysha: Truth; fact; reality; noble

*Aliza: Joyous; happy; cheerful

*Amatullah: Female slave of Allah

*Aminah/Ameena/#Amina: Trustworthy; faithful; truthful

*#Amirah/Ameera: Princess; leader

*#Aneesa/Anisa/Anisha/Aneesah/Anisah: Friendly; good company; close; intimate; affectionate

Aqilah: Intelligent woman; wise; prudent

Aqsa: Enclosed by the walls; inside

*Areebah/Ariba: Sharp; quick; intelligent

*Areej: Pleasant aroma; sweet smell

Aroob: A woman who is devoted to her husband; loving wife

Arshia: Divine; heavenly

Asalah: Purity; nobility

*Aseelah: One who is from a good family

*Asiya: One who takes care of the weak

Asma: More eminent; precious; daughter of the first Khalif

*Atif: Generous; kind; sympathetic

*Azeeza: Cherished; honoured; valuable

B

Baasima: Smiling; cheerful

Baheera: Bright; luminous

Bahiyaa: Pretty; beautiful

Basheera: One who brings good news

Basma: A smile

Benazir: Incomparable; unique; Benazir Bhutto was the Prime Minister of Pakistan and the first female Prime Minister of an Islamic state

Bushra: Good omen; happy news

Buthayna: Wonderful; delicate

D

Delisha: One who makes others happy; one who gives pleasure to others

Dhuha: Forenoon; morning

E

Ereshva: Righteous; just

Esita: Desired; wished for

ℱ

Faatina: Charming; attractive; fascinating; enchanting

Fadeela: Virtuous; righteous; moral

*Faiza: Victorious; successful

Falak: Star

*#Farah/Farha: Joy; delight; pleasure

*Farhana: Happy; cheerful; glad

*Farheen/Farhina: Happiness

*Faridah/Fareeda: Unique; incomparable; precious pearl; derived from the Arabic word 'farada' which means 'unique'

*Farihah/Fareeha: Content; joyful; glad

*Farzana: Clever; bright; wise

*Fatimah/Fatima: Accustom; withhold; one who weans; the name of the daughter of the Prophet Muhammad, who was known as the 'Mother of all Muslims', who weaned all children

*Fawziya: Successful; triumphant

Firdaus: Paradise; garden; beautiful place

Firoza: Turquoise; precious stone; gem

*Fizza/Fiza: Nature

*Fizzah: Silver; pure

𝒢

Gazala: A deer

Ghaada: Beautiful; good looking

Ghaaliya: Fragrant; aromatic; scented

Ghaydaa: Young; adolescent

Ghusoon: Branches of a tree; shrub

Gul: Rose; a flower

H

*Haadiya/Hadiya: Guide to justice

*Haala: Fame; halo around the moon

*Habiba/Habeebah: Beloved; dear; another name for the holy city of Medina

*#Hafiza: Protected; guarded

*Hafsa: Young lioness; cub; the wife of Prophet Mohammed

Haifa: Slim; one with a beautiful body

*Haleema/Halima: Gentle; patient; calm

*#Hameeda: One who is worth appreciating; praiseworthy; admirable; derived from the word 'hamid' meaning 'thankful' or 'praising'

*Hana/Hannah: Happiness; bliss; delight

*Haneefa: One who has full faith in Allah

Hanima: A wave

*Haniya/Haniah: Delighted; happy

*Hasina: Nice-looking; beautiful

Heer: Diamond; jewel

*#Henna: Also known as Mehndi, Henna is applied to an Indian bride's hands and feet and is a symbol of good luck in married life

Hessa: Fate; fortune

Hooriya: Angel of paradise

*Huma: A bird which brings joy and prosperity to people; lucky bird

Humaila: Golden necklace; precious

*Husna: Beauty; a girl

I

Ibtihaaj: Joy; pleasure

Ihina: Enthusiasm; interest; eagerness

Inas: Social; communal; one who shares with everybody

Inaya: Concern for others; kindness

Intisaar: Triumph; victory; success

J

Jahanara: Crown of the world; queen of the world

Jala: Charity; aid; donation

***Jameela/Jameera**: Good-looking; attractive

Janaan: Heart; mind

***#Jasmin/Jasmine/Jazmin**: Name of a fragrant flower used to make perfumes

Jumaana: Pearl; gem; jewel

***Juvariah/Javeria**: The name of Prophet Mohammed's wife

K

Kaamla: Ideal; faultless; perfect

Kaia: Firmness; stability

Kameela: Most perfect

Kanizah: Young slave girl; servant

***Kareema**: Kind; dignified

***#Kareena**: Pure; clean

***Khadeeja/Khadiza**: Premature child; the first woman to accept the religion of Islam; the first wife of the Prophet Mohammed

Khairiya: Charitable; helpful

Khalida: Immortal; eternal

Kouther: A river in paradise

Kulthoom: Daughter of the Prophet Mohammed

Kyna: Wise; clever

L

Lamees: Soft skinned; delicate

*Lateefa: Gentle; tender; sociable

*Leena/Lina: Devoted one; tender

M

*Madeeha: Praiseworthy; admirable; commendable

Mahajabeen: Good-looking; gorgeous

*Maheera/Mahirah: Expert; skilful

*Mahfuza: Protected; secure; cared for

*Mahmuda: Praised; admired

*Maimoona: Auspicious; blessed; the wife of the Prophet Muhammed

Maisa/Maysaa: Stylish walk; walk with pride

Majeeda: Dignified; respected

Malak: Angel; messenger

*Maleeha: Charming; graceful

Malka: Queen; princess

Manaal: Achievement; accomplishment; success

Maraam: Goal; aim; objective

Mariyah: Fair complexioned; one of the wives of the Prophet Mohammed

Maryam: Maidservant of Allah; mother of Isa

Maysoon: One with pretty features

Meeza: Crescent moon

*Meher/Mehereen: Compassionate; empathetic

Mehrunissa: Tendancy to do good; kindly

Mufeeda/Mufida: Beneficial

Muhja: Soul; heart

Muna: Wish; desire; derived from Arabic word 'maniya' meaning 'to desire'

*Muneera/Munira: Illuminating; shedding light; luminous

Musheera: Advice; give an opinion

N

Naaz: Pride; grace; style

*Nabeeha: Intelligent; noble; wise

*Nabeela: Very generous; highly open handed

Nada: Dew

*Nadia/Nadiya: Beginning; the first

*Nadira: Rare; precious

Nadwa: Council; board; committee

*Naeema/Naima: One who has the blessings of Allah for a happy life

*#Nafeesa/Nafisah: Precious; jewel

#Nagma: A style of song

*Nahida: Eminent; superior

*Naila: Acquirer; obtainer

*Naimah/Nahima: At ease; comfortable

*Najaah: Success; victory

Najeeba: Intelligent by birth; of noble birth

*Najiya: Secure; protected

Najla: Broad eyed

*Najma: Star; valuable

Najwa: Private conversations

Naseen: Cool breeze

Nashida: Learner; student

Nashita: Full of life; lively

*Nasiha: One who gives valuable advice; sincere counsellor

Nasira: Helper; assistant

*****Nasreen**: Another name for the Jonquille flower

Nawal: Present; gift

Nawar: Flower; blossom

Nazaaha/Nazeeha: Purity; virtue; honesty

*****Nazeefa**: Unsoiled; clean

Nazeera: Equal; similar; identical

*****Nazeeya/Nazia**: One who thinks positively; optimistic; hopeful

Nazimah: Poetess; manageress

***#Naznin/Nazneen**: Delicate; tender

Nikhat: Fragrance; aroma

Nimaat: Blessings of Allah

*****Noor/Nour**: Light; angel; derived from Arabic word 'nawara' meaning 'to illuminate'

Noorien/Nooreen: Light; bright; shining

Noorjehan: Light of the world; derived by combining 'noor' and 'jehan' meaning 'light' and 'the world' respectively

*****Nosheen**: Good in taste; sweet; happiness

Nouf: Peak of a mountain

Nudhar: Gold; precious; valuable

Nuha: Wisdom; mind

*****Nusrat**: Help; aid

R

Raaida: Chief; leader

Raawiya: Storyteller; transmitter of ancient poetry or stories

Rabab: White cloud

Rabeea: The onset of spring; garden; the fourth one

Radhiyaa/Radeyah: Content; satisfied

Radhwa: Name of a mountain in Medina

Rafa: Divine healing; happiness; prosperity

*Rahimah: Graceful; elegant

Raniya: One worth staring at; gazing

Rasha: Young gazelle

#Rasheeda: One who is correctly guided; wise; intelligent

Raya: Flow; full with drink

*Reema: A deer

*Rihana: Sweet basil

*Rizwana: Satisfying; fulfilling

*Roza: Flower; rose

Rubaina: Bright; brilliant

Ruksana: Brilliant; radiant

Ruqaya: Rising; growing; the name of a Prophet's daughter

Rutva: Dialogue; speech

Ruwayda: One who walks quietly

S

Saabira: Patient; tolerant

Saaliha: Of use; helpful

*#Saalima: Safe; secured; healthy

Saamiya: High; prominent

*Saba: Early morning breeze

*#Sabena: A woman from Sabine

Sadiqua: Honest; sincere

*Sadiya: Blessed; fortunate; lucky

#Saeeda: Priestly; religious

*Safa: One with clear and pure thoughts; peaceful

*Safiya: Calm; best friend; faithful

*Sahiba: A woman

Sahila: Lead; direct

Sahira: Mountain; awake

Sahla/Suhayla: Smooth; fluent

Sahna: Shape; appearance; look

Sahoj: Strong; tough

*Sairah: Traveller; tourist; voyager; explorer; holidaymaker

*Sajida: Lying flat, face downwards to Allah; worship

*Sakeena/Sakinah: Divine serenity; auspicious calmness

Salena: The moon

*#Salma: Calm; quiet; peaceful

Saloni: Gorgeous; stunning

Salwa: Shrink back; comfort

Samaah: Kindness; compassion

*Samar: Evening chat; talk at night-time

*Samara: Mountain; derived from 'samaria', which means 'watch mountain' in Hebrew

Sameeha: Kind; liberal

*Sameena/Samina: Healthy; fat

*#Sameera/Samira: Entertaining companion for chat

*Samiya: Exalted; important

*Sana/Sannah: Radiance; splendour

*Sara/#Sarah/*Sareena: Princess; lady; Sara was the name of the wife of Abraham in the Old Testament

Sayeeda: Leader; head; manager in charge

Shaadiya: Singer

Shabab: Beauty; prettiness; splendour

Shabana: One who belongs to the night; young lady

Shabnam: Dew

Shagufta: Flowering; blossoming

Shaheena: Falconess

*Shahnaz: Pride of the king; derived by combining 'shah' meaning 'king' and 'naz' meaning 'pride'

Shakeela/Shameena: Beautiful; good-looking

Shatha: Fragrant; perfumed

*Sheena: Gracious gift from Allah

*#Shirin: Sweet; pleasant; lovely

*Simran: Remembrance; the sweet remembrance of Allah

Suha: The name of a star

*Sultana: The dignified empress; queen

*Suraya: Many stars; derived from the word 'thuraya' which is another word for the Pleiades, a group of seven stars in the constellation of Taurus

T

*#Taahira: Virtuous; pure

*#Tabassum: Smile; laughter

*Tahsin: Praise; adornment

#Taranum/Tarannum: Melody; tune; derived from the word 'tarana' meaning 'song'

Taroob: Cheerful; joyful

*Taslima: Obedient; compliant; dutiful

*Tasnim/Tasneem/Tasnima: Finest drink; the name of a heavenly fountain of divine wine

Tehzeeb: Manners; etiquette; style

Thanaa: Gratitude; appreciation; praise; admiration

Tharaa: Assets; property; capital; funds

Thuraya: Seven stars; another word for the Pleiades, a group of seven stars in the constellation of Taurus

U

Ulfah: Companionship; love; harmony

Urooj: Elevation; altitude; high

Uzma: Supreme; superior

W

Wafeeqa: Successful; unbeaten

Wafia: Trustworthy; loyal; faithful; derived from the word 'wafa' meaning 'truthfulness'

***#Waheeda**: Distinctive; unique; single; sole

***Wajeeha**: Eminent; prominent; notable

Warda: Rose; flower

Wateeb: Heart

Wijdan: Feelings; ecstasy; opinion

Y

Yafiah: Tall; high; towering

Yakoota/Yaqoot: Emerald; gem; valuable

Yasirah: Easy-going; lenient; ease of a wealthy life; rich

***Yasmeen/#Yasmin/Yazmin**: Jasmine flower. A beautiful and fragrant flower from the Olive family. Yellow Jasmine represents grace and elegance; white Jasmine repesents amiability and Spanish Jasmine represents sensuality. Dreaming of the Jasmine flower is said to be an omen of success in romantic or personal affairs

Z

Zaafira: Prize-winning; successful; firm

#Zahida: Ascetic; abstinent; one who keeps away from all kinds of pleasure

#Zahira: Shining; radiant

***Zahraa**: White; fair in colour; daughter of the Prophet Mohammed

*Zahrah: Beauty; a flower in bloom

*Zaina/Zayna: Beautiful; pretty; good-looking

*Zainab/Zaynab: Name of a flowering shrub; name of a Prophet's daughter

*Zakira: One who worships Allah regularly

*Zakiyaa: Honest; truthful; straightforward

#Zarina/Zarine: The golden one

*Zeena: Wisdom; intelligence

*Zeenat: Decoration; adornment

Zehba: Gold; precious

Zenobia: Father's pride; name of an ancient queen

#Zubeda: The best; the top one

Zuha: To sacrifice; 'Id ul Zuha' is the festival of sacrifice and is one of the most important Muslim festivals – it is called by the name of 'Bakri-Id' in the Indian sub-continent

*Zuleika/Zuleyka/Zulaikha: Brilliant; beautiful

Muslim Twin Names

Boy – Boy

Amir – Zaahir

Armaan – Salman

Ashraf – Musharraf

Asim – Nasim

Azim – Nazim

Javed – Naved

Javed – Waahid

Kaif – Saif

Majid – Saajid

Rahim – Karim

Rehman – Irfaan

Zaahid – Waahid

Boy – Girl

Amir – Amirah

Anees – Aneesa

Saajid – Saeeda

Salman – Salma

Girl – Girl

Aminah – Sabena

Farah – Sarah

Henna – Zarina

Nafeesa – Hafiza

Nagma – Salma

Rasheeda – Hameeda

Sabena – Kareena

Sameera – Saalima

Shirin – Naznin

Taranum – Tabassum

Waheeda – Zahida

Yasmin – Jasmin

Zahira – Taahira

Zubeda – Zahida

Sikh Names

In India, a person's last name is often an indicator of caste. Sikhism rejects the idea of a caste system because people of certain castes are considered to be superior to people of other castes. In order to develop a system where all are equals, the tenth guru of the Sikhs gave all men the last name of 'Singh' meaning 'lion', and all women the last name of 'Kaur' meaning 'princess'. As a result, all Sikh names can be used for either girls or boys. This way, no one can tell a Sikh's caste from his or her name, and all Sikhs look upon one another as equals.

A

Agam: God; Lord; almighty; one who is unapproachable

Agampreet: Love for God; derived from the word 'preet' meaning 'love'

Akaldeep: The eternal lamp; God's lamp which burns continuously; derived from the combination of two words 'akal' and 'deep' meaning 'endless in time' and 'lamp' respectively

*Amandeep: One who brings peace; derived from the words 'aman' meaning 'peace' and 'deep' meaning 'lamp', thus literally meaning 'lamp of peace'

Amanjeet: One who achieves peace; derived from combining the words 'aman' meaning 'peace' and 'jeet' meaning 'to win'

*Amanpreet: One who loves peace; derived from 'aman' meaning 'peace' and 'preet' meaning 'love'

Amardeep: The lamp of immortality; one who is immortal; from 'amar' meaning 'immortal' and 'deep' meaning 'lamp'

Amarjeet: Always victorious; derived from the words 'amar' and 'jeet' meaning 'immortal' and 'victory' respectively

*Amarpreet: Immortal love; everlasting love; derived from the combination of the words 'amar' meaning 'immortal' and 'preet' meaning 'love'

*Amrit: Spiritual holy water; nectar; drink which makes one immortal; according to the Indian myth Mahabharata, Amrit was made in the ocean during Samudra Manthan (ocean churning)

*Amritpal: The name of one who becomes immortal by drinking Amrit (see above)

Atamveer: Brave; courageous; fearless

$\mathcal{B}$

Balbir/Baldev: Strong; mighty; well built; valiant hero; derived from the word 'bala' meaning 'strength'

*Balraj: Powerful king; derived from two words, 'bala' and 'raj' meaning 'strong' and 'king' respectively

Balvinder/Balvindra/Balavant: Strong; one of the many names for the God Hanuman, renowned for his strength in the mythological epic Ramayana; Balvinder and Balvindra are derived from Balavant

Barindra: The ocean; sea

Bhagat: Devotee of God; Bhagat Singh was a legendary Indian freedom fighter who sacrificed his life for the cause

Bhupinder/Bhupinderpal: Preserved by God; one who is looked after by God himself

Bishanpal: One who is brought up by God

C

Chamkaur: The name of the battlefield where the Sikh God, Guru Gobind Singh, fought

Charanpal: Protection under the Guru's lotus feet

Charanpreet: One who worships the Lord's feet; one who has faith in the Guru

$\mathcal{D}$

Dalbir: Courageous soldier within his group; derived by combining two words 'dala' and 'bir', meaning 'group' and 'brave' respectively

Daljeet: The conqueror of forces; 'dal' meaning 'group' and 'jeet' meaning 'victory'

*Dara: Wise; clever; compassionate

Deepinder: God's light; God's teachings; derived from the words 'deep' meaning 'light' and 'Inder' referring to 'Lord Indra'

Devendra: King of Lords; chief of Gods; derived by combining the words 'Dev' and 'Indra' meaning 'God' and 'Lord Indra' respectively

Devjeet: God's triumph; God's victory

Dharamdeep: Lamp of religion; one who keeps the religion going; one who spreads religious teachings to others; formed by combining two words 'dharam' meaning 'religion' and 'deep' meaning 'lamp'

Dharampal: Supporter of religion and religious values

Dharmender/Dharmendra: Lord of religion; one who is religious; the base word is 'dharam', meaning 'religious person'

E

Ekanjeet: God's triumph

Ekanpreet: Love for God

G

Gagandeep: Light of the sky; derived by combining 'gagan' meaning 'sky' and 'deep' meaning 'lamp' or 'light'

*Gurdas: Slave to the Guru; formed by combining 'Guru' and 'dasa' meaning 'Guru' and 'slave' respectively

*Gurjeet: One who wins the Guru's trust; triumph of the Guru

*Gurjeevan: One who lives life like a Guru (ensuring spiritual progression, promoting the glory of Sikh history, abstaining from the use of intoxicants and non-vegetarian food, keeping the bodily form intact, etc); formed by combining words 'Guru' and 'jeevan' meaning 'Guru' (the God) and 'life' respectively

*Gurleen: One engrossed in the Guru and his teachings

Gurneet: Guru's morals; morals given by the Guru

*Gurpreet: One who adores and respects the Guru and his teachings

*Gurudeep/Gurdeep: Lamp of the Guru; one who throws light on the Guru's teachings; one who spreads the teachings of the Guru

*Gurveer: Warrior of the Guru; one who fights for the Guru

*Gurvinder/Gurinder: The Guru; the God

H

Harbhajan: Lord's devotee; hymns sung for the Lord; derived from the words 'hari' and 'bhajan' meaning 'God' and 'hymns' respectively

Harbir: Warrior of God; one who protects the religion

*Hardeep/Harjyot: God's light; Lamp of the God; God's teachings

Harinder: Lord

Harjeet: The God's triumph; victory of the God

*Harkiran: The God's ray of light; the God's path of life

*Harleen: One who is engrossed in the God, his teachings and the religion

*Harmeet: A friend of the God; derived from combining the words 'hari' meaning 'Lord' and 'meet' meaning 'friend'

Harpal: One who is protected by the God

*Harpreet: One who loves the Lord

Hartej: Radiance of the Lord

*Harvir/Harveer: Brave Lord; one who is brave like the God

I

Inderbeer: King of bravery; Lord's soldier; a combination of 'Inder' referring to Lord Indra and 'beer' meaning 'the brave one'

Inderjeet: The conqueror; God's triumph; derived from 'Inder' referring to Lord Indra and 'jeet' meaning 'victory'

*Inderpal: One looked after by the God

Inderpreet: Love for the God

J

Jalender/Jalindra: Lord of waters; full of water; derived from the word 'jala' meaning 'water'

*Jasdeep: The light of God's glories; one who spreads and carries forward the Guru's teachings

*Jaskiran: The ray of light shown by the Lord; the Lord's teachings

*Jasleen: One who is absorbed in the teachings and knowledge of the Lord

*Jasmeet: The Lord's friend, companion

Jasminder/Jasvinder: Lord's glory; the Lord of Glory

*Jaspreet: One who praises the fame and glory of the Lord

*Jasraj: Lord of fame; king of fame

Jaswant: Praiseworthy; admirable; victorious

Jitender: Conqueror of Indra; derived from the word 'jita' meaning 'conquered'

Joginder: Unification with God

K

Kanwaljeet: Lotus; the Guru's lotus feet

*Karanveer: Brave; courageous

Khushwant: One who is happy, joyful, contented; derived from the word 'khush' meaning 'happy'

Kirpal: Kind; merciful; generous

Kuldeep: Heir of the family; derived from the words 'kul' meaning family of generations and 'deep' literally meaning 'light', but interpreted here as 'heir'

Kuljit: One who brings victory to the family; heir of the family

Kulveer/Kulvinder: Hero of the family; the brave soul

Kunwarjeet/Kuwarjeet: Prince; youth

M

Mahinder: God of Gods; derived by combining the words 'maha' and 'Inder' meaning 'superior' and 'Lord Indra' respectively

*Mandeep: Light of the mind; lamp of the heart; from 'mana' meaning 'mind' and 'deep' meaning 'light' or 'lamp'

*Manjit/Maneet: One who wins everybody's heart

*Manpreet: One whose mind and heart are full of love

*Manraj: One who is the king of his own mind; one who listens to his own mind

*Manveer/*Manvir: One who is brave; courageous; mentally strong

*Manvinder: God of mankind

Mohinder: Variant of Mahinder, meaning 'great Indra'; derived from the Sanskrit word 'maha' meaning 'great', combined with the name of the Hindu God, Indra

N

Nanak: The only one; derived from the combination of two Sanskrit terms, 'na' and 'anak' meaning 'not-but-one'. Guru Nanak was the first of the ten Gurus of the Sikhs, and is considered to be the founder of the Sikh religion. Guru Nanak was the embodiment of Divine Light

Narinder: Derived by combining the words 'nara' meaning 'mankind' and 'Inder' referring to Lord Indra, Narinder means 'king of all mankind'

Navjot: The new light; a radiant person; derived from 'nava' meaning 'new' and 'jyot' meaning 'flame' or 'light'

Navneet: A lively person; forever fresh; innovative

Nihal: One who is happy, cheerful

P

Paramjit: The greatest victory

*Paramveer: The greatest warrior; 'param' meaning 'great' and 'veer' meaning 'the brave one' form the name Paramveer

Parmeet: The greatest friend; the best friend

Parminder: The greatest God

*Pavandeep: The sacred light; the spiritual teachings of the religion; formed by combining the words 'pavan' meaning 'sacred' and 'deep' meaning 'light'

Praneeta: Led forward; conducted; advanced; promoted

Puneet: Pure; sacred; divine

R

Raghubir: Another name for Lord Rama from the Indian myth, Ramayana

Rajender/Rajinder: King of the Gods; emperor

*Rajpal: A king who protects his kingdom

*Rajveer: A brave soldier of the kingdom

Ramandeep: One who is engrossed in the light spread by the Lord; one who is absorbed in learning the Lord's teachings

Randeep: The light of the battle; the hero of the battle; derived from the words 'rana' meaning 'battlefield' and 'deep' meaning 'light'

Ranjit: The winner of the battle; one who conquers the battle-field

Ratan: Gem; jewel; one who is precious; Ratan Tata is the chairman of the Tata empire, India's largest and best-known Indian conglomerate, established in 1887 and comprising 85 operating companies

Ravinder/Ravindra: The sun God; the God of knowledge and wisdom; derived from the words 'ravi' meaning 'sun' and 'Inder' referring to Lord Indra

*Rupinder/ Roopinder: The God of beauty; the most beautiful one; derived from the words 'rupa' meaning 'beautiful' and 'Inder' referring to Lord Indra

S

Santa: A highly dignified person; a glorious person

Sartaj: The crown of the head; the chief; a person in charge

Satinder: God of truth; one who always speaks the truth; derived from the words 'satya' meaning 'truth' and 'Inder' referring to God Indra

Shamsher: One who is courageous and fearless like a lion; derived from the word 'sher' meaning 'lion'; another name for a sword

*Simran: One who is engrossed in the Guru and his teachings; meditation

*Sukhdeep: The lamp of happiness and pleasure; one who brings happiness and joy to everyone; derived from the combination of 'sukha' meaning 'happiness' and 'deep' meaning 'lamp'

Sukhwinder: The God of happiness

Sundar: One who is good-looking; beautiful; handsome

Surjit: The triumphant God; the successful one

T

*Tajinder: God of splendour; the God's greatness

Takhat: Throne; supreme power; there are five Takhats (thrones/governing powers) in Sikhism – Akal Takhat, Patna Sahib, Keshgarh Sahib, Hazoor Sahib and Damdama Sahib. Akal Takhat is considered supreme, and decisions concerning the entire Sikh population of the world are taken in the Akal Takhat. Decisions made by the other four Takhats can only be applicable after getting the approval of the Akal Takhat

Tanvir: Strong; physically powerful; muscular

Taran: The saviour; a boat

Tejbir: The radiance of the brave one
Tekjot: One who believes in the teachings of the Guru
Thakur: Guru; God; Lord; leader

U

Uddham: Consistent effort; a diligent attempt
Ujjal: Bright; pure
Upjeet: A splendid triumph
Upraj: A gracious king
Uttam: A glorious and dignified person
Uttamreet: Glorious lifestyle; high standard of living

V

Veerindar: Brave Lord Indra; one as brave as the God
Vijender: God of victory
Vikramjit: A heroic victory; a praiseworthy triumph

Y

Yashpal: Protector of fame; derived from the word 'yash' meaning 'fame'; Yashpal Sharma was a famous Indian cricket player who played for the country from 1979 to 1984

BABIES' NAMES A-Z

Your child's name is important – it has got to last for life! To help you make the right choice, André Page has compiled particulars of more than 3,000 names. Some have been in use for centuries, some are modern or American names, while others are Anglicized variants of names common in Europe. André explains what each name means, as well as giving some historical or modern examples of famous people who share the name.

THE NEW A-Z OF BABIES' NAMES

Jacqueline Harrod conducted extensive research among the recent registers of births at the Family Records Centre to produce this book, focused on the most popular names of today, along with some traditional favourites and a few unusual ones. The result is almost 1,000 names in A-Z sequence, each featuring fascinating background information, including meaning, derivatives and famous holders of the name in history, literature and legend.

Uniform with this book

More books for parents from Elliot Right Way Books

THE EXPECTANT FATHER

Betty Parsons shows how parents-to-be can share the magic of childbirth through *understanding*. Whether or not you plan to be beside your partner at the birth, as prospective father you are the best placed person on earth to give her the growing comfort and confidence she is going to need. This deliberately dad-centred book prepares you to maximise that support.

C-A-T = CAT

Teach Your Child To Read With Phonics

If your child is about four years old and ready to start reading (or is older but among those still being held back), you can and must do something about it *yourself* straightaway. This *phonic* method will show you how; by sounding out the letters of each word, building up words and sentences, line by line, left to right, *you* can teach your child to read.

Uniform with this book

RIGHT WAY
PUBLISHING POLICY

HOW WE SELECT TITLES

RIGHT WAY consider carefully every deserving manuscript. Where an author is an authority on his subject but an inexperienced writer, we provide first-class editorial help. The standards we set make sure that every **RIGHT WAY** book is practical, easy to understand, concise, informative and delightful to read. Our specialist artists are skilled at creating simple illustrations which augment the text wherever necessary.

CONSISTENT QUALITY

At every reprint our books are updated where appropriate, giving our authors the opportunity to include new information.

FAST DELIVERY

We sell **RIGHT WAY** books to the best bookshops throughout the world. It may be that your bookseller has run out of stock of a particular title. If so, he can order more from us at any time – we have a fine reputation for "same day" despatch, and we supply any order, however small (even a single copy), to any bookseller who has an account with us. We prefer you to buy from your bookseller as this reminds him of the strong underlying public demand for **RIGHT WAY** books. However, you can order direct from us by post or by phone with a credit card.

FREE

If you would like an up-to-date list of all **RIGHT WAY** titles currently available, please send a stamped self-addressed envelope to

ELLIOT RIGHT WAY BOOKS, BRIGHTON ROAD, LOWER KINGSWOOD, TADWORTH, SURREY, KT20 6TD, U.K. or visit our website at www.right-way.co.uk